Babouche Impromptu and Other Moroccan Sketches

Clara Hsu

AF271570

E T
O R
P Y
Hotel
Press

ISBN: 978-0-9891578-3-4

Library of Congress Control Number: 2013918171

Poetry Hotel Press
P.O.Box 347063, San Francisco, CA 94134-7063
www.poetryhotelpress.com

To Dore Steinberg
who taught me the art of travel

ACKNOWLEDGMENTS

A warm thank you to Lynn Werner who offered insightful comments and suggestions, and Al Averbach for copy editing.

My gratitude extends to Dan Brady, Don Brennan, Sydney Clemens, Vern Peralta, Winnie Poon, Noemi Sohn, and Vince Storti, whose support and friendship made this book possible.

Front cover photo by Saul Edwards.
Sahara photos by Ken Aoki.
All other photos by Dore Steinberg.
Clara's portrait at Camondo Steps, Istanbul, Turkey by Pat Moran.

CONTENTS

SKETCHES

POEMS

AFTERWORD

The Sand

The hourglass tips. Sand escapes from the narrow opening. I don't see the hourglass, only its mouth, a hole somewhere in my brain and the sand keeps pouring.

Fast and furious obscuring my sight sucking me into its momentum taking the body out oh no we don't need that body. I move with the sand, moving forward or maybe backward depending on how you look at things.

Once you let go it takes only seconds to reach millennium and there's no stopping. Someone appears in my periphery something looks like a mud wall but I'm blurred by the speed of motion and the sand.

Two brown skinned men, sunken eyes, weathered faces in dirty white turbans and indigo robes. Between them a pinky girl in ragged dress. Arms down her sides, her big eyes stare as the sand rain down. I ride through her hair and she feels me as the wind but seeing them I know at once this is where I was.

Only too much sand had come between us.

October 2003

Traveling in Morocco began as an incidental vacation with my friend Dore Steinberg. In the end I found myself drawn to the inhabitants of the Arabic tongue.

Between Moroccans

A quick knock on the door of our train compartment and a young Moroccan lilted in. He was in his twenties, clean-shaven and casually dressed in sweat-shirt and jeans.
"May I sit here?"
"Of course," Dore, my companion replied.

The train to Fez started from Marrakech at 5:30 in the morning. It was now afternoon and we would be arriving in about an hour. The Moroccan sat quietly for only a moment.

"My name is Mohammed. You're from America? How nice. I would like to go there someday."

We'd gotten used to this conversation opener in the three days we spent in Marrakech. Most of the time it was merchants luring tourists for business. Mohammed's English, however, was impeccable. A student at the university in Fez, he wanted to go into the tourism business. Mohammed was disappointed that we planned to stay in Fez for only one day.

"Have you gone to the Atlas Mountains? The desert?"
No. We haven't.
"Bring her to the desert," he turned to Dore, "it's the most romantic place on earth. It's the place to fall in love...I can take you there."

We looked out the window to the pouring rain.
"Perhaps another time."

But Mohammed insisted in mapping out our one day in Fez. He suggested a family run riad that had just been renovated. He would take us into the famous maze-like souk. He would invite us to his home and meet his mother and sisters. In the evening, he would bring his uncle Ali to play music for us. He would even arrange a taxi to take us to our next destination,

Chefchaouen, a small town north of Fez.

How far did Mohammed go in his helpfulness before asking for compensation? It never happened. Mohammed delivered everything he promised. His price was friendship, and a t-shirt off Dore's back. The next morning promptly at 9, a taxi arrived at our door.

Our driver Idriss was a slender man, balding, and with a big mustache. He wore a well worn white shirt and grey pants. We hopped into his patchy old car. Right from the beginning there was a funny noise every time he turned his steering wheel. Idriss assured us that the car needed some attention, but it would make the three-hour trip.

Driving down a tree-lined road, the sun was peeking out of the thick clouds.

"Idriss, are you a Muslim?" Dore asked.
"Yes."
"We love the calls to prayer."
"Yes. We pray five times a day."

A flock of sheep appeared in front, swamping half the road. The shepherd waved at us.

"You eat a lot of lamb in this country," said Dore.
"Oh, anytime we have a celebration, we sacrifice a lamb. Birthdays, weddings..."
"I wonder if the lamb feels sad to be picked as the animal for sacrifice."
"No," said Idriss," the lamb is joyful to be picked by Allah."
"How do you know?"
"It's in the Koran."
"Do you know the Koran well?"
"Yes of course."
Idriss turned to me and asked where I was born.

"Hong Kong."

Idriss beamed. He reached over and took out two Chinese opera cassettes in his glove compartment.

"You like Chinese opera?" I turned to him, amazed.

"Yes. These were gifts from two ladies from Taiwan."

We had gotten used to the squeaky steering wheel when Idriss pulled the car over and stopped. One of the tires was punctured. He didn't have a spare.

A small local bus came into view. It was jammed with passengers. When they saw Idriss with the tire they stopped and squeezed him in.

The sky began to drizzle. Dore and I looked out to a ditch surrounded by a grove of trees and soft rolling hills in a distance. We huddled and slept. Two hours later Idriss reappeared with his repaired tire.

By the time we reached Chefchaouen it was almost three o'clock in the afternoon. Hungry and tired, we invited Idriss to have lunch with us before he headed back to Fez. Idriss pulled the car into a parking lot. As soon as we walked out of the car, three men approached Idriss. They circled him. One of the men, round face and heavyset, did most of the talking. Idriss looked helpless and shook his head repeatedly. A few more men saw the commotion and came over. Now with an audience the interrogation became fierce. I jumped in at a moment when everyone was catching their breaths and asked Idriss what was the matter.

"They won't let me go into town. They think you've hired me as a tour guide for Chefchaouen. I told them I'm only the taxi driver, but they won't believe me. It's illegal to guide if you don't have a license."

The round face man and company smiled condescendingly when Idriss spoke to me in English. Obviously they didn't want to offend the tourists, but they weren't going to let Idriss off the hook.

"You're mistaken. Idriss is our friend. We want to take him to lunch," I ignored their smiles and spoke to them earnestly. The men had no idea what I was saying.

Idriss translated, but the men weren't satisfied. Their voices got louder and more menacing.

"Let's go to the police," I said, getting hyped up from the situation.

"They *ARE* the police," Idriss said despondently.

"Ask them for identification then. No good police would bully people like this," I continued, when a loud but thin, raspy voice cackled behind my back.

"Lady, please don't get involved in this. This is between Moroccan and Moroccan."

I turned around and saw a tiny gnome of a man with a big, black umbrella. He looked about forty-ish, wearing an off-white woolen cap and matching d'jellaba. I was glad to see another person who spoke English.

"No!" I was adamant, "You must tell these people that Idriss is not our guide, and that he will have his lunch with us before he goes home."

The gnome stepped in. After some negotiations Idriss was released from the grilling, but not before more threats were thrown at him as the crowd dispersed.

We walked into town, trembling under our outwardly casual pace. Our shoulders almost touching, drawing on each other's courage, conscious that people were watching us.

"They'll come after me when you are gone," Idriss was depressed and worried.

"We'll walk you to your car after lunch," said Dore, and

Idriss' spirit picked up a little.

After lunch, Idriss helped us with our luggage and settled us in a hotel. We said a fond goodbye in the parking lot and watched him drove away unharmed.

The next day, we saw the gnome perching on his black umbrella on the exact same spot where the argument took place. We greeted each other heartily. While Dore was adjusting his camera, the man turned to me. What happened the day before still troubled him.

"You shouldn't have gotten into the discussion yesterday. It was between Moroccan and Moroccan."

"It had nothing to do with Moroccans," I replied, "It was between human being and human being."

Our gnome friend looked down the dusty road. His bright eyes were now sparkling. Moving his free arm and feet as if he was dancing, he swooned in his high-pitched voice, "Yes, yes!" Then steadying his umbrella on the ground and with one foot set on a tree stump, he posed with me smiling into the camera.

February 2007

Three and a half years later I sold my business, ended a long marriage and became a poet. After studying Arabic for a year I returned to Morocco, this time alone.

Cradle

Africa,
we are locked in each other's consciousness.
You, vast, ancient, magnificent in blue
call me,
who long ago tumbled out of your bosom
into faraway lands.

Oozing the scent of exotica,
your messengers lead me
through labyrinthine trails.
I shed my skin
layers of translucent doldrums.

Your sequined dress billows
golden lips chant a lullaby
ochre arms enfold the first of my dreaming
take it back to a time
when I was very small.

Some Arabic Words:

meh-kanee-mooshskeel —no problem
medina—old city
l'hoyer—my brother

Meh-kanee-mooshskeel

In the semi darkness I slowly massaged my back. It had been hurting even before my journey. The long flight from San Francisco together with an eight-hour delay at the Heathrow airport intensified the pain.

I'm in trouble.

Yet I was exhilarated when tiny lights draped across a darkened land came into view.

I'm back! Back to the country that had stolen my heart. How it beckoned me, in dreams and through meeting a steady stream of people who had been to Morocco. I yielded to this intangible feeling, this sudden love and curious obsession by returning, alone, without a plan.

Besides the back pains, the logistics of getting to my hotel also gnawed at my mind. I had booked a room at the Hotel Medina two months ago by telephone. It would be somewhere in the medina, the old city of Marrakech, not far from the famous D'jamma Elfna Square. My original plan was to take the local bus to the square and search for the hotel. But now we would be landing late at night. The bus might not be running and I was reluctant to take a taxi. I had been warned that taxi drivers in Marrakech were known for extorting inflated prices from tourists. At night I would clearly be at a disadvantage.

An old man had been conversing in Arabic behind me throughout the flight with his neighbor, a plainly dressed young man who was attentive, translating his needs to the stewardess. I considered my situation for a moment and decided to approach the young man. My heart pounded as I turned around and introduced myself. But the man, Aziz, was friendly and ready to help. I asked him if he knew anything about the bus.

"I never take the bus so I can't help you there. My friends are picking me up. If you don't have too much luggage, we could give you a ride."

Aziz assured me that it was not out of his way. He had been working in London and he was returning to visit his mother.

"*L'hoyer,* my brother," he spoke into his cell phone, an animated conversation ended with a nod towards me.

The old man sat quietly until he realized I could speak a few words in his language. He told me his name was Saiid and his daughter would be coming for him.

The plane touched down in Marrakech. We walked down the aircraft's metal staircase into a balmy night. While waiting at customs, Saiid spoke to Aziz earnestly, turning his head towards me. Aziz made a gesture. His fingers touched his forehead and then the heart. In a short time, my new friends had taken up the role of guardians, ensuring my well-being on arriving in their country.

Outside the airport two men were waiting for Aziz. Saiid's daughter ran to the old man and gave him a big hug. She brought children and husband and some other relatives and friends. The entourage thanked Aziz warmly and moved on, chattering happily as they disappeared into the night.

Aziz introduced me to his friends. They shook my hand and said, "Meh-kanee-mooshskeel."

What did it mean?

"It means 'no problem,'" they explained.

As we drove, the scenery became familiar. I remembered the landmarks, pointing at the grand hotel La Mamounia on the right. Soon after the famous Koutoubia, a simple rectangular minaret came into view. It bathed gracefully in the lights. I wondered aloud if D'jamaa Elfna had changed much.

Aziz smiled, "Three years is nothing. If you come back fifty years from now D'jamaa Elfna would still be the same."

We arrived at the entrance to the square. Aziz opened the trunk and took out my luggage.
"Are you sure you'll be all right?" There was concern on his face.
"Yes, I am," I straightened up slowly." Thank you so much for your kindness."
"Not at all. I would want people to do the same for my sister when she needs help."

Aziz put his hand on my shoulder and gave it a pat. I turned, and with my luggage vanished into the crowds of flowing robes.

More Arabic words:

hammam — public bath house
d'jellaba — long sleeved, loose fitting hooded garment
riad — an enclosed garden courtyard
inshallah — if God wills

Suaad

The entrance to the medina was at the far end of D'jemaa Elfna Square. An archway led into a narrow street brightly lit with souvenir shops. Young Moroccan men sat in front of the shops on low stools, their eyes moving with the crowd and spotted a target quickly.

"Hello, where you from?"
"Big welcome. Would you like to see my shop?"
"Japon? Korea? Wait! I want to ask you a question."

A motor bike roared and pedestrians pressed their bodies to the walls. They resumed their brisk pace and darted around more vehicles and donkey carts. I kept my head up looking for signs, hoping I would find my street soon.

Street signs were sporadic in Morocco and often hidden behind something more useful, like a ladder, or a provisional business. It was an ecstatic moment when the script sidi bouloukat appeared high on a wall in front of me. I mumbled the name over and over with a big grin, savoring every letter, proud that my struggle in Arabic was paying off. Hotel Medina triumphantly appeared half way down the lane. I walked in. The man on duty couldn't find my reservation. They had no room for the night.

"Meh-kanee-mooshskeel," he said as he took my luggage across the lane to the Hotel Aday. It was clean, basic and cost the same.

"Meh-kanee-mooshskeel," I said.

My tiny room contained a bed and a sink. A window with wooden shutters opened out to a central courtyard. Flowery blue ceramic tiles decorated the floors and the walls. Voices of returning guests and late arrivals echoed in the concrete building well into the night. Now, alone and relaxed, every movement—sitting, bending, lifting, was filled with pain. Every turn on the bed was excruciating. Sleep came slowly.

The next morning I consulted with the receptionist, Hasan, to see if I could get a massage.

"The hammam is closed. It won't be opened for a few days. You can go to the spa. Fatima will show you."

Fatima, a small woman in headscarf and d'jellaba came out behind Hassan and led the way. The spa was just down the next street in a traditional Moroccan house. Two French ladies ran the operation. It had a riad, an enclosed garden courtyard. The place was stylishly decorated with indigenous artwork and filled with the aroma of essential oils.

I told the French ladies I had a terrible back problem but they just showed me the price list in French. I pointed to the 45 minutes "relax" massage as that was the only word I recognized. One of them called out a name. A young, bespectacled Moroccan woman came downstairs. Her long dark hair was pulled back into a ponytail. Her starchy ash-pink uniform—short sleeved top and long pants—accentuated her slightly bulging midriff and hips. I followed her into a room upstairs, where she asked me to undress. When I introduced myself in Arabic, she was surprised and pleased. She said her name was Suaad.

Suaad placed paper towels on the massage table. I climbed onto it stiffly as my back muscles twitched painfully with every movement. She poured oil on my back and worked on it gently. She laughed lightly as she tried French on me and got nowhere. I summoned all the Arabic I could remember and told her where I live, the names of my two children, and what I like to eat. Most of the time it was a guessing game on both sides, but eventually we understood each other. Suaad said she had two young girls. Her husband was a coiffeur, hair stylist, in the medina. While she worked, her mother looked after the children.

I wanted Suaad to work harder on me. I pushed my palm down on the table hard, pressing on it. She smiled but I could tell she didn't understand my gesture. She asked me to turn over. I got up half way when my back muscles started to spasm and I whimpered. Suaad gave me a big nod and asked me to lie down again. Now she bore down with her whole body, arms pushing and palms digging deep into my sides, kneading, stretching, and ironing out the tendons. The stuffy room grew warm. I could hear her breathing accelerate.

When she finished I told her I might come back the next day for another massage. She agreed I would benefit from a double treatment. Suaad led me back to the courtyard. There, I was given a glass of lukewarm mint tea and a sugar cookie. One of the French ladies set a selection of lotions and oils on my table and walked away. The price tags were outrageously expensive. Suaad kept smiling at me but went to a corner table and sat with the other women who worked there. The atmosphere was strictly business. I felt uncomfortable with the clear division between employers, employees, and customers and left quickly.

I slept much better that night and did not wake until almost noon. The spasm had relaxed. I made an appointment for the afternoon. This time, I selected a bath and massage package.

A young woman took me to the rooftop and into a small enclosure that had two little adjoining rooms. After I stored my clothes in the dressing room, she led me into the steam room. A long couch was set against the wall. Next to it two faucets ran hot and cold water continuously into a terracotta basin. I scooped the water with a half gourd and poured it on myself as I sweated in the heat. Meanwhile the woman took off her uniform. Her small breasts and slender body fitted pleasingly into a multi-color bikini. She rubbed gooey soap on my body and applied some kind of mud afterward. Then she scrubbed me down with a rough hand mitten. Dead skin rolled up into soft black flakes and rinsed off. She applied henna to my hair. My body relaxed into the heat, steam, hot water and the fragrance of herbal extracts. What a luxury it was to be washed like a baby, steeped in the pleasure of touch.

Suaad appeared in the doorway after my bath with a big

smile. She noticed right away that I was better, and proceeded to give me the same massage. When she finished, beads of perspiration ran down her face and hair, steaming up her eye-glasses.

I told her I wanted to leave for the desert soon, and wondered if we would see each other again. She said she may not be working at the spa for very long.

"Why?"

"I am pregnant and showing. They don't want a pregnant masseuse."

Gazing at her drenched face, I considered her exertion on me, her need to work for the family, and imminent dismissal. There was no resentment or anxiousness in her voice and manner. Her nature was that of a person who looked upon hardships with equanimity.

"They pay us very little here, very little," Suaad confided, "but I can't get customers by myself. Maybe I'll go to America some day, *inshallah*. Do they pay masseuses well?"

I assured her that, with her skills, she would do well in America. She put her two index fingers side by side and rubbed them along each other.

"We're friends," she said.

*

I left the spa and took a long, slow walk, past D'jamaa Elfna Square, around the landmark minaret Koutoubia, into a garden. Roses and a variety of flowers flaunted their resplendence under the warm sun. A line of trees shaded the walkways. They were jasmine. Their thick, sweet scent saturated the air. The tiny white flowers were hardly visible in the green foliage, but I knew they were there.

More Arabic words:

henna — A reddish-orange dye
harrira — hot soup
tagine — stew
pastilla —a pie with shredded chicken wrapped in warka
dough, sprinkled with powdered sugar.
kufis — a white cap
dirham — Moroccan currency
Mez'yena — good
shukran — thank you

A Cosmic Symphony

D'jemaa Elfna—the pulse of my heart. Your air is
perfumed with incense mixed with the smell of grilled meat.
Motorbikes criss-crossing pedestrians, blind beggars' sing-song
among flowing robes and snake charmers' circular arm motions
bring me to you. On hot sunny days, you stall me with the line of
giant burgundy carts, with oranges stacked full in wire baskets. A
young man in a white shirt pours me a tall glass of orange juice.

Lizards, scorpions, oils, bones and dried animal parts
in translucent skin of camel's kneecaps are the playthings of
blue-turbaned Berbers. Let me smell the burning sage and muse
at your aphrodisiac Berber Viagra. Let me see the henna patterns
you carry in your hands, oh women of D'jemaa Elfna, and watch
out for your needle pumped full, ready to squeeze a design on
my arm.

Late afternoon cookout, plumes of smoke rise from pots
of boiled lamb heads, spiral shell snails and spicy harrira soup.
Arm grabbing men with menus run down the list:
  fish
  shrimp
  calamar
  beef
  chicken
  mixed grill
  tagines
  pastilla
  aubergine
and free mint tea you know Moroccan Whiskey? Come come sit
down sit down right here big welcome.

D'jemaa Elfna I'm mesmerized by your circles of people,
the passionate speeches of men and acrobats somersaulting on
hard grounds. I'm drunk after a cup of hot ginger tea that softens
my stiff Chinese upbringing and lets me dance. Dance to the re-

lentless drumming, to the rhythms of Africa, in the center of the universe where life is a cosmic symphony that goes on without end.

*

A cross-section of Africa gathered around the performers; an amalgamation with a single intention: to be entertained. They were mostly men. Their skin color varied from light roasted almond to deep midnight. Some wore kufis and djellabas, but most of them wore casual cotton shirts and pants. They stood close to each other with little expression, carrying small change in their pockets for the end of the shows, and for anyone who came up to them with an outstretched hand.

In one of the big gathering circles a stout man with a red bandana plucked his banjo and sang passionately. Behind him sat a chorus of drummers, boisterous, echoing and bouncing musical phrases at each other. Then all at once, as if the musicians noticed the audience for the first time, they saluted the crowd. The banjo player urged everyone to make a tighter circle, teased them for crossing their arms to protect their pockets. The chorus agreed and started praying to Allah, "Perhaps money would descend from heaven?"

The banjo player walked slowly in front of each spectator. From the compressed bodies money imperceptibly changed hands. Now he became more vehement, threw the few dirhams he collected on the ground and preached with profound gesticulation on the art of generosity.

I looped around to catch glimpses over the shoulders of men as the circle was four to five people deep. One of the drummers discovered me. He waved cheerfully and gave me a chair to sit in the front.

In one of his rounds the banjo player came close to me and whispered,

"Would you like to hear Berber music?" I noticed his face, rugged with furrows. He smelled of dust and sweat.
"Yes, I would."

He stepped away and continued with his sermon, but suddenly burst into song. A couple of old women nodded their heads and clapped with the music. Just as everyone was getting into a groove, the banjo player stopped and started his speech again.

I motioned him over.
"If I give you 20 dirhams, would you kindly play a longer piece?"
"No," he said, smiling, "no."

I suddenly understood his preaching was part of the act.

Across from this big production a young woman sat with an ancient man on a piece of cardboard. The old man looked like a dark chocolate sculpture with deeply wrinkled skin and perfectly toothless gums. He was plucking on a small lute that was hardly audible, and his partner tapped on a make-shift drum. I put a dirham on their tray. Suddenly the duo became utterly animated as if they were wind up dolls. The old man puckered his mouth. His eyes twinkled like a child's, and strummed the instrument madly.
"*Mez-yena, mez-yena*—good, good," I clapped.
"*Shukran, shukran*—thank you, thank you," the young woman nodded happily.

A singular voice distracted me. I broke from the couple and searched for the voice. It was coming out of another big circle. Men were packed shoulder to shoulder. Here on the outer ring, a gruff-looking old man stood motionless, leaning against a biker whose foot was frozen on the pedal. I paused next to them and craned my neck to see what was happening. A storyteller was "stretching his tongue." Unlike most of his counterparts who wore colorful robes and turbans this one dressed plainly in shirt and pants. He had no prop. The audience was intent on the monologue. Men's jaws were loosened; their eyes hardly blinked. Mesmerized, these people might have been standing here for hours, days, or maybe centuries bound by the magic of words.

At first he articulated each syllable slowly. His voice rose in increment as the words gathered momentum, soaring rapidly to a high point, then trailed like a kite tail in the air. He paused, marked the silence, turned and suddenly exploded. A long string of rhythmic verses followed the outbreak, sizzled as if they were in a pot of fire. The storyteller put his hands to his head. His eyes were wild but steady. His focus was directed to one man in the crowd. The man looked confused, having being singled out. The storyteller spoke with earnestness to the man, sometimes entreating, sometimes harsh. He put his fists together and made believe they were shackled. He threw out a question. No one answered. He grew irritated and asked another question. A hundred eyes stared back. There was a look of triumph on the storyteller's face. He knew he had his audience. Now he could mold and shape their hearts and minds, knock their wind out, or drive them into a dizzy frenzy.

The storyteller's voice spiraled and pounded in my direction as though he was questioning me. His husky and seductive litany touched a darkness that was lurking as I saw myself coming upon a solitary adobe hut, small, round, ashen against the night. As I walked toward it, the storyteller's voice turned strident.

... I can't go in...there's no door, no window... it's a funeral mound...

He was now whispering, urging. Our eyes met.

I stepped back.

More Arabic words:

souk — market
kaftan — a loose fitting overcoat
babouche — Moroccan slippers

The Old Medina

Mid morning, blue sky, red walls and the promise of another warm day. I decided to explore the residential area of the old medina, get lost if I had to. Starting from one end of the souk, past a school that had turned into a museum, tiny nameless streets began to sprout from the main thoroughfare. This was the starting point for me.

The streets were lined with little shops selling everyday wares. School children in blue uniforms waved at me. Some came running up close, shouting, "Ah-low, ah-low." They giggled and laughed, prancing around me, regrouping behind my back. Women in checkered patterns and colorful d'jellabas or kaftans shopped together in couples or groups. People crossed the streets expertly, darting between moving vehicles. Some of the streets weren't paved. Regardless, cars sped down kicking up the dust. Their exhausts puffed out black soot.

It must have been afternoon when I felt tired and decided to look for a place to sit down. Walking around several parked rusty bicycles, I noticed a man who came out of a hole-in-the-wall joint. In his hands he carried a tray laden with an array of food in clay dishes. They looked and smelled delicious.

I peeked into the tiny space. A few men were having lunch. The cook at the counter motioned me in. I sat next to an elderly man who had a solemn expression on his face. He didn't acknowledge my presence but when I pointed at his bowl he ordered for me. It turned out to be a spicy lentil and lamb tagine with bread and a tomato salad. A woman brought out cups of water for each customer. My neighbor drank his and wanted more. I pushed my water to him. He accepted it without a word.

We finished our lunch at the same time. I said goodbye to everyone and walked on. Suddenly I heard a ring behind my back. It was my lunch buddy on his bike. He waved at me and nodded with a sunny smile as if he had come across an old friend.

Checking my compass, I had wandered away from D'jamaa Elfna going east. In order to go back, I headed west into a small street. White-washed walls stood tall on both sides. Metal doors at predictable intervals gave the feeling that these were dwellings. Children's laughter and adult voices occasionally drifted from inside the walls. I twisted and turned from one narrow lane to another; wondering when I would get out of the maze. A man appeared at the next corner. He was bending down opening his door. When I asked, he assured me I was not too far from the square. He stepped half-way into the door but came out again.

"Keep to your right. Don't turn left at the next corner."

With this crucial information D'jamaa Elfna's surrounding wall appeared in front of me in no time.

The souk leading back to D'jamaa Elfna was strewn with garbage: vegetables and meat scraps, donkey excrement, paper, plastic wrappings, and other unidentifiable but definitely putrid objects. At every corner I could expect yet another heap of rancid materials. Squatting against a wall, men and women displayed lettuce and potatoes on plastic sheets. Some of them had only a couple of tomatoes or a few bunches of parsley to sell. Butchers were cutting away, separating organs and intestines in their little cubicles. Scrawny cats sauntered about waiting for fresh scraps. The slightly sweet smell of blood wafted over to the colorful scarves and souvenirs hanging on the racks across the street. On one side, a man was waving a fly-chaser made out of long palm leaves over his honey cakes. Further down, rows of babouches, soft pointy leather slippers juxtaposed with shiny brass tables and lanterns. Shoppers strode at a snail's pace, comparing and bargaining for the same merchandise that could be found in a hundred other shops. Donkey carts and motorbikes jammed the street going in both directions. The clopping hooves and rapid-fire exhaust pipes together with merchants hawking their wares charged the air. When the entire company reached a critical mass, everything came to a standstill.

A boy of eight or ten stood peeling a tangerine in the middle of all the activities. The peels fell from his hand onto the pavement; bits of orange gold dotted the ground. I paused when a man in d'jellaba walked out from the side of the street and put his hand gently on the child's shoulder. The boy looked up. The man extended his other hand towards the floor, and I became aware of the orphaned amber, abandoned emerald and outcast ruby— onion skin, parsley stalks and pomegranate seeds— that peeped from the crevices of the streets, hidden behind wooden crates or huddled in a ditch. Unwanted little jewels. Life's accidental confetti.

Ice Cream

The European travelers were dressed for the sun. They swamped D'jamma Elfna, arriving in droves from France, Germany and the UK: backpackers, tour groups, as well as parents and children. Many wore sleeveless shirts, shorts and spagheti-strapped tops. Bare shoulders, arms and legs strode among long robes and covered faces. The genuine everyday living of the Moroccans suddenly seemed like a Hollywood movie set. D'jamma Elfna had turned into a backdrop, a virtual playground designed to please the visitors.

I saw a line of tourists gathered around an ice cream stand on my way back to the hotel. Children were noisily pointing and choosing their favorite flavors. I decided to join them. As I was waiting for my turn, a young local boy came up to me. He politely asked if I would buy him an ice cream. "Sure," I said. The boy ordered a chocolate ice cream.

Someone tapped my back before I could scan the selections. It was a little girl. She couldn't have been more than six years old; dark skin contrasted against her white T-shirt and blue pants. Her black tight curls pulled up into two small plaits; big eyes spoke quietly under her knotted brows. In her hands she held two packages of tissue paper. I gathered she might be a novice peddling in the square. Obviously she wanted an ice cream too. I asked the boy if he would share his ice cream with her. He said yes. The sales lady brought out a plastic spoon.

The little girl shook her head slowly. She didn't want to share. Her resolute face asserted the right to the entire ice cream, cone and all, just like the other children in line. I placed my order and when I turned around she was still standing there. Her pupils darkened, glazed by a thin watery film. Her lips pressed into a line. The little girl was determined not to cry and in that instant she transformed. Her rectitude loomed over me and demanded total surrender. The ice cream felt awkward in my hand.

I gave it to her and left.

An Experiment

Evening. After a meal of fried calamari and chickpea soup at the square, I noticed several kiosks on the edge of the big cook-out. The men inside these little booths were pouring dark amber liquid into small glasses, and cutting small chunks off a huge mound that looked like chocolate mousse. They put the portions on plates. I went up to a customer at one of the kiosks and asked him what he was drinking.

"It's ginger," he said.

I ordered a cup and decided to try the mousse too. The drink was incredibly strong. The mousse was a mixture of ginger and spices. It had a chalky texture and an intense flavor. I worked at both slowly. The smooth tonic traveled down, warming my stomach. Just as I finished the last sip, the attendant leaned over with his kettle and half filled my glass and the other customers'.

"It's free," he said cheerfully. Out of politeness I finished the drink, and walked away slightly intoxicated. Perhaps the spices had heightened my senses. A wave of giddiness came over me. The crowd parted, and I found myself standing in front of the ancient-looking lute-player from the other night. This time he was without his young partner. Sitting on a cardboard he plucked his instrument softly and no one paid attention to him. When he saw me, his eyes lit up in recognition. He proceeded to sing and play.

I had the feeling people were curious about my delight in watching the old man play, because they looked back and forth from me to him. Now a thought came to me: I wanted to see how big a crowd I could gather for the man. I kept smiling and nodding, and he kept playing. This went on for a long time until I couldn't pretend to enjoy this musical phrase anymore. He felt the disconnection from me right away and came to a stop with a grand trill on the last note. People clapped and the crowd broke up. The old man shook his head and waved his hand. It occurred to me I might have exhausted him. Perhaps he did not need this excitement. I bent down to say *shukran* and felt a bit uncertain whether I had done a good or bad thing.

The Local Bus

Hasan the receptionist woke up when he heard me dragging my luggage down the stairs. His eyes were puffy with sleep. "When you come back, remember this is your home."

I thanked him and walked to the square. D'jamaa Elfna stood empty of activities. The grounds had been cleaned. Puddles of water reflected the early morning light. A couple of snakes and men idled at their usual spot. They were the only remnant from yester-night.

A taxi was waiting. The driver approached. I asked him how much it would cost to go to the bus station.
"Twenty dirhams," he said.
I shook my head and kept walking.
"Fifteen dirhams," he yelled.

Another taxi pulled up. This time I told the driver through the open window how much I would pay. He nodded and I got in.

A man at the ticket window led me to my bus. He asked for twenty dirhams "for the luggage". I didn't have exact change and gave him a hundred dirham note. He ran back to the office to get change. I waited for a long time. Just as I thought I would never see him or my money again, he came back with a swathe of bills in his hand.

The local bus was shaggy like an old donkey, with tattered carpet and worn seats. I sat in the front half of the bus and watched passengers slowly get on board. As we waited, a self-assured young man appeared next to the driver's seat. He wore a western-styled jacket and carried a leather briefcase. Instead of the short tight curls common among Moroccan men, his hair was wavy and styled. When he saw that a good number of people had settled down, he began to speak. The young man told his captive audience he knew how tiring it was to sit in a bus. You could get a headache, joint ache, back ache, and even nausea. Well, he had just the right remedy. He struck a pose; right hand casually touching the lapel on his jacket before dipping into his pocket and pulled out a small packet. A camel logo was prominently stamped in the front. This, he held up for everyone to see, would ensure a smooth ride. He opened the packet and took out some droplets sealed in plastics. As an incentive, he would give a free sample to the first customer. He walked down the aisle, handing out small pieces of paper written in Arabic, but he didn't give one to me. I gathered these were leaflets to validate his claims. A man came up to him and bought two packets. A few others did the same. Satisfied, the young man collected the leaflets from the passengers, packed up, and left.

Before long a woman wearing old clothes appeared. Her diminutive body was weighted down by a sleeping child strapped on her back. She twisted her hands together and wailed a heart-wrenching speech. Almost everyone in the bus opened their purses to her. Then a rough-looking man approached clumsily from the rear of the bus. His big frame brushed the elbows and shoulders of the passengers as he moved. Since most of us had already given, he received only a few dirhams from the late arrivals.

Now the bus started rolling but stopped almost immediately at a gas station. A blind beggar approached while we waited for the tank to be filled. The bus attendant brought the man into the bus. He walked the length of the aisle with the man. Afterwards he took the beggar by the elbow and escorted him out of the bus, giving him a pat on the back.

There was no air conditioning so all the windows were partially opened. The bus made several stops in the city. It began to fill up. I moved over to the window seat. A young woman who looked like she was from the rural area sat down next to me. She wore a pale green cotton headscarf and tied an additional red-checkered kerchief tightly around her nose and mouth.

She seemed aloof, not ready for interaction. I offered her some cookies. She took two but did not eat. After about an hour she unwound her face cover and reached into her robe. At first I thought she might be taking food and wondered if she would offer me a treat in return, as it was customary to share with your neighbors.

She pulled out a clear plastic bag, put her mouth to the opening and started to vomit quietly. The bag was half full of yellow liquid when she stopped. I pulled out a small cup of water from my bag and asked if she wanted it. She took the water and stood up. With one fling she threw the bag of vomit over my head out of the open window. Then she sat down to drink the water. When she finished she stood again and threw the plastic cup out.

The Atlas Mountains were dotted with rocks. Wild-flowers of lilac shade bloomed like a light stroke of watercolor. I imagined her vomit spilling onto the ground would eventually dry up, but the plastic bag and cup might be caught by the stem of a blossom, flapping limply in the wind.

Desert Rookie

The young Japanese man had short hair, a thin mustache and goatee. We noticed each other at one of the rest stops. Aoki Kensuke (Ken) was in his mid-twenties, between jobs, and had two-months to travel. When he realized we both were going into the desert, Ken asked if I would like to look for a tour with him. I liked his quiet manner and easy-going attitude and said yes.

We arrived at Zagora, a desert town on the outskirt of the Sahara. The bus conductor had suggested that we visit a tour office in town, and we were able to settle on a three-day tour with little trouble. Early next morning, a young Berber greeted us at the entrance of the tour office. He looked just about five feet tall. On top of his tiny face was a bright yellow turban, partially covering a head of black curly hair. When he smiled he flashed a set of teeth stained yellow, brown and a deep rusty red. His white desert gown reminded me of a Mexican poncho, except this one was made with light cotton, and the front and back corners on either side were tied together in a knot. A few of his toenails were painted red.

"This is Youssef, your guide," said the manager of the tour office.

Youssef led us to a minivan. After an hour of bumpy ride, Youssef motioned us to get out. The driver climbed to the roof of the bus and threw down our sleeping bags. I saw two camels resting across the road. A tall, lanky young man wearing an indigo turban and a deep sky-blue *khamees* greeted us. This was Omar, our other guide. Next to him were four big basketfuls of supplies.

The place where we started our journey was strewn with cans and plastic bottles. Ken picked up a big piece of glass and showed it to me. He quietly put it into his knapsack. After about an hour, we came upon a shelter. Wooden posts and mud walls held up a canvas woven with camel hair. It was enclosed on three sides. Youssef and Omar set down the sleeping mats and carpet, transforming the sandy shelter into a living room.

"We'll rest here," said Youssef.

Omar passed around some oranges. We opened the thick rinds with our fingers. Youssef threw his rinds out of the shelter.

"No!" I exclaimed, thinking of all the garbage on the sand.

"Sorry, sorry," said Youssef.

The rinds landed in front of the camel. He gobbled it up right away. I apologized to Youssef for my rash reaction and expressed my dismay at the polluted surrounding. Then I took my rinds and threw them to the camels.

"Youssef, is this really the Sahara?" I was a little disheartened.

"Not yet. You'll see. We'll come to a big gate with the word Sahara across, just like Disneyland," Youssef waved his arms in a half circle as he spoke.

"With welcome signs in Chinese and Japanese, I bet," I lightened up.

"Yes. You won't miss it," he said, giving me a serious look.

Youssef pulled out a tea set: a metal pot and four small glasses set on a tray. He showed me the tea.

"It's from China."

After water was boiled, he threw a couple handfuls of tea into the pot.

"Ken, look into the basket and find the sugar," he said.

Ken had never seen how Moroccans made their tea. He thought the sugar might be in a small box or paper bag. Rummaging through the basket, he pulled out the flour and all kinds of spices but couldn't find the sugar.

Youssef laughed.

I told Ken, "Look for a big white brick."

Ken uttered a string of exclamations in Japanese as he pulled out the sugar brick from a black plastic bag. Youssef broke a big chunk off the brick with his knife and dropped it into the pot. After the sugar dissolved, he poured the tea into a glass and back into the pot three times. Now it was ready to be served.

Youssef and Omar had been friends since childhood. They often displayed a familial intimacy sprinkled with laughter when speaking to each other in their Berber language. Like children taking on a grown-up role, they were attentive to their customers yet playful at the same time. Over lunch we found out Ken and Youssef were the same age, with Omar one year younger. Ken had bought some hashish in Tangier. When he took it out to share, he was inducted into the "family" right away.

I told Youssef and Omar my 51st birthday would be the second day of our tour. Omar objected vigorously.

"*La, la!*—no, no!" He kept saying, "You are teasing us. My mother is 50 and she is walking with a cane already."

"But I live like a bebe and I'm sure your mother works much harder than me."

"Life in the Sahara is hard, but not difficult," they philosophized. They both had big families with lots of brothers and sisters. Youssef was born and raised in the Sahara. His mother and grandmother made jewelry and his father would take the trinkets into town to trade for food. After his father died it was impossible for the women to take care of nine children (six of them were daughters) and so they moved to Zagora.

The trail of garbage gradually disappeared as we continued our journey after lunch. There had been rain a few weeks ago. Wildflowers sprouted from the sand. Black and red berries, lilac and white flowers, tiny string beans hanging from baby green branches, and yellow cactus flowers stuck out like fat beeswax candles. My camel, who had been walking obediently, couldn't resist the feast. He bent down and pulled the plants out of the ground, eating everything in sight. Youssef wouldn't let him dawdle. We had to find a place to camp before sundown.

We came to a small flat area among the sand dunes and pitched camp. Youssef bent one of his camel's front legs and tied a rope around its leg and thigh. The camel got up and hopped around with three legs. Omar did the same with his.

"If a camel wanders off he can't find his way back. We do this so they can't go too far," explained Youssef.

Ken and I rubbed our backs. We had been rocking back and forth when riding on the camels and hadn't mastered the rhythm. I told Omar about my bad back. He gestured me to brace myself. Standing from behind he lifted me by my elbows and gave a quick jerk up and down. My vertebrae clicked into alignment. He picked Ken up and did the same. We were instantly "fixed."

Youssef and Omar began to prepare dinner. I had not peed all day so I asked Youssef where I could go to the bathroom. Youssef gave a quizzical look. I could see the absurdity of the word in this setting. So I tired hammam, which in Arabic can also mean toilet. Youssef and Omar looked at each other. By now I was a bit desperate. I had to be explicit.

"I want to go pee."

"What's that?" They asked as they washed the vegetables.

Ken was enjoying this little comedy but really couldn't help me. I got up and said to Youssef, "I'm leaving."

There was concern on his face as he thought I was angry with him. Then all of a sudden he realized what I wanted and tossed me a roll of toilet paper. I asked him what to do with the toilet paper afterwards. He threw his lighter to me.

"Burn it," he said.

I walked a good distance away from the men and peed, when suddenly I realized I didn't know how to work the lighter. After several futile attempts I headed back to the tent.

"Youssef, I know I'm crazy."

"*La, la.*"

"Yes, yes. I don't know how to use your lighter."

Ken laughed so hard he rolled on the floor. Youssef flicked the lighter and gave it to me to try. I imitated him, moving my thumb over the little gear on top of the lighter. No flame came out. Now the men fell on top of each other like dominos, gasping for air.

"Harder, harder!"

Finally it sparked and lighted. I took the lighter back to my "spot" and burned the piece of toilet paper. When it turned into ashes, I pushed sand over it.

After sunset and before moonrise there was a long period of complete darkness. Once in a while a shooting star scratched the dark canvas, leaving a fingernail mark that was quickly erased. We waited. A pale light emerged from the horizon. It spread wider and wider until suddenly the moon floated gracefully up and lighted the sky.

"The moon seems so close you can grab it by the hand," said Omar.

Now we could see our surrounding. Youssef and Omar talked among themselves. The camels had wandered off. Omar invited Ken to go with him to bring them back.

*

A semi-circle of white candles glimmered in the sand. All was quiet.

I went into the tent and stretched my back on the mat. Youssef came in. When I sat up, he moved behind me and began to massage my back. His touch was light and gentle. I turned around to thank him afterward but he held me with an intensity that was suggestive.

"I like you." His dark eyes gazed at me under the loose curls.

"Youssef, you are half my age. You could be my son!"

"That's not how I see you," he said, solemnly, "Your face is very beautiful to me, and I feel you are a very good person."

I didn't know how to handle this unexpected situation. He seemed sincere. It would be wrong to reproach him.

Youssef was silent now that he had revealed his feelings. He stood up and suggested that we go outside. We walked up the sand dune. The air was crisp and cool. Youssef's energy was renewed. Sitting side by side he turned to me and said something in Arabic, that I am his love. When I questioned him, he would not repeat it.

"Youssef, we can be friends."

"May I touch you?"

"Yes."

Befuddled by my own answer, I grew pensive. Youssef moved closer. He caressed my back. Then with a sigh he touched my hair and planted two kisses on my cheek.

"You have beautiful hair."

I realized things might have gone a bit too far.
I turned to him and said in a firm voice, "Youssef, I am a very strong woman and enjoy being alone."

He heard me and stopped.

Amid our awkward silences, Youssef muttered numerous "hamdullah". I said little. After a while he went down to the camp to build a bonfire and make tea. I stayed up, saddled on the edge of the dune, hoping out of the vast darkness there would be wisdom. I wondered if Youssef was the kind of guide who gave women tourists "special" attention in order to gain financial or sexual access. It would be very unpleasant if that was the case because Ken and I had to depend on him for the next three days.

Somehow, I felt Youssef's expression was genuine. I was not threatened by him and decided to let things unfold.

Just as tea was ready, camels and men showed up. The atmosphere turned noisy and rowdy in an instant. Ken told me Omar seemed to be able to see for miles with the aid of a tiny flash light. Youssef made a comfortable chair for me from the camel's mount. In front of the bonfire we drank tea. Omar wrote our names in Arabic in the sand. I sat contently and watched the three young men saying silly things to each other, sharing cigarettes and hashish well into the night.

A Birthday Party

Morning. I climbed out of the tent and examined the tracks on the sand dunes. They gave suggestions of beetles, lizards, birds, and snakes, crisscrossing like connecting lines on a celestial chart. On closer look, there were hoofs and paw prints. I watched my clumsy, heavy feet rake up their delicate impressions. With the sun rising, the critters must have gone looking for shade. Today was my birthday. Aside from an occasional bird call and the gurgles of camels, the quiet, fresh like the clear blue dawn, suited a new beginning.

After breakfast we went on foot across a dry riverbed. Stones and pebbles covered the ground, a treasure trove of black and gold banded nuggets, dark green rock panels serrated by the wind, silken mauve and gritty gray sandstones compressed together; heaves of boulders, hooves, horns, and little white bones. Omar walked at an unhurried pace in his rubber slippers with the grace of a man at home in his environment. He was always in the lead and would occasionally blurt out a Japanese phrase to Ken. They seemed to enjoy each other's jokes very much.

Youssef and I were slower in the back. He picked up a small stone with black and brown layers and gave it to me. Ken and Omar were a clear distance ahead. Youssef looked at me and asked for my hand. I hesitated. His hand outstretched. Without a second thought I put mine in his.

Sunlight drenched the great plain. In the searing heat we trudged on until we came upon a large Acacia tree. It spread out like a huge umbrella and provided much needed shade. Youssef and Omar began to prepare lunch, but the wind had intensified, and soon it became impossible to keep the fire on the stove. The men put the tent up and moved the equipment inside. I walked around the area looking at the stones and found an unusual one. It had two different textures and a purple streak ribboned around it. I showed it to everyone. They all thought it was a good stone.

After lunch, Youssef and Omar took a nap under the Acacia tree with blankets over their heads. Ken and I sat on the mats in the tent. We bore the waves of sweltering heat by minimizing our movements, like lizards hidden under a rock. My eyelids grew heavy; even blinking took effort.

The wind was still strong when the worst of the heat had passed. While Youssef was taking the tent down, I looked at the stones on the ground again and found two more that attracted me. I showed them to Ken and Youssef.

"This one is a heart," Youssef pointed to the ash green stone.

"And this one looks like a map of the world," suggested Ken.

I took out the purple-ribboned stone. It now looked like a shoe to me.

Walk with your heart in the world.

These rocks were my birthday gifts from the Sahara. I was sure of it.

Toward evening, we settled in an area with many trees. Omar gestured for me to come closer to him. He folded Youssef's long yellow turban, which had been tied on his camel's neck all day, and wound it around my head.

"This is a present from Youssef for your birthday. He wants you to have it."

I looked over to Youssef, who was busy peeling tomatoes and preparing couscous for dinner. When I thanked him he gave me a tiny nod.

Ken had mixed sand and water and made a big round cake. On the cake stood four hashish cigarettes which he had carefully wrapped the night before. Youssef and Omar were more excited about the smoke-able candles than the inedible birthday cake. Youssef lit them immediately. Omar gave me a knife to cut the cake. We posed for pictures. It was a good thing Ken had a camera.

Omar handed his gift to me. "Where did you get this?" I laughed, as a pair of huge plastic ski glasses unraveled from a paper napkin tied with a red string.

"From a Swiss tourist," he replied.

After a feast of soup and couscous, Youssef lay down to rest. Omar and Ken built a bonfire. The branches were dry. They burnt out quickly. I went here and there to gather some more twigs to keep the fire going. Youssef got up without a word and went behind our camp. Soon he came back with three huge trees, bare and brittle. I sat down. The men broke the branches and threw them into the fire. The flame shot up instantly with sparks reaching up to the tree I was sitting under.

"Youssef, the fire is too big. It may incinerate us all."

"*Inshallah.*"

Omar went to sleep, but Youssef sat quietly with me. When I turned around to open my sleeping bag, he shoved sand into the fire and buried it.

Origin

> *I wake*
> *with the moon framed by the Acacia tree*
> *a diamond sparkles in her hair.*
> *I wake again, the sun has risen*
> *and moon but a shadow in the pale blue sky.*
> *Under a cactus I wash my face*
> *dry it with a nomad's scarf.*
> *My nails are blackened, my hair is matted*
> *My blouse dusted with golden sand.*
> *Sing. Sing! With flies buzzing about*
> *dung beetles leading the way,*
> *sing!*

Pale green shrubs gleamed in the morning sun. I wiggled out of my sleeping bag and looked around. The men were sleeping soundly. I wandered among the vegetation, and followed a little dung beetle busy marking lace-like trails across the sand. When I returned Omar was already making fried bread.

"For your first day after your birthday," he offered the first piece to me. The bread was crispy on the outside, slightly chewy and soft inside.

*

Youssef took off his white Berber gown and put it on me. Not long after we started our walk he asked for my hand again. We walked for a short distance when I let go of him and said, "*Ila, ila*—go, go." Youssef looked inquisitive, but quickly accepted the fact that I wanted to be alone. Now with camels and men in front of me, I reflected on sand and stone, man and nature, and my growing fondness for the young nomad.

We came to a well. Under Omar's supervision Ken let down a canvas bucket and filled our water containers. We settled a short distance away. While Youssef and Omar made lunch, Ken and I went back to the well and helped each other wash. We shampooed our hair. The cold water was refreshing after three days of not washing.

Youssef and Omar went for a wash after lunch. They came back with a change of clothing. Omar put on a light blue long tunic, which made him look princely. He asked for my mirror. Peering into the glass intently, he heaved a sigh and shook his head. Omar gave the mirror to Youssef while lamenting something in Berber. Youssef looked at himself carefully too, and had the same resigned expression as Omar. The two had an unusually quiet moment.

Ken took a walk. When he came back he was carrying a plastic water bottle he had filled with sand. He wanted to bring it back to Japan as a souvenir.

"Aw! You'll go to jail for this," Omar exclaimed dramatically, "The Saharan sand cannot be taken. You can bring bones and rocks with you, but sand? No!"

"Why, Omar?"

"Because of the color," Omar continued, "It's a bigger offense if they find you carrying sand than hashish."

Omar went on for a while, alternating serious and threatening faces with his ridiculous reasons. When Ken wasn't looking, he turned to me and shook his head vigorously, mouthing, "Just kidding, just kidding!"

Youssef and Omar did not take a nap. We drank tea and shared our life stories. I was curious about their enterprise and asked them about their camels. After some calculations converting the dirhams into yens and dollars, we came up with an astronomical figure.

"It's the cost of a Mecedes Benz," Youssef finally thought of a comparison, "except you cannot mate a Mecedes. A camel is more valuable."

"Where are the ladies?" I asked.

"They are home with the babies. Only male camels come out to work. It is natural," replied Youssef, "I grew up with tourists. A lady from Switzerland invited me to visit her. I didn't want to go. This is my home. I want to be with my family," he continued.

"I surf the Internet when I'm not working," said Omar. He wrote down his e-mail address for Ken and me. I asked Youssef for his.

"I don't write," he said, but told Omar to give me his home address.

We came to the great sand dunes on our last night. While Ken settled on the ridge to watch the sunset, I ran down to the bottom of one dune and up another, imprinting my feet on each crest, spoiling the windblown wrinkles on the dunes. Childishness possessed me. I stomped, rolled, made angel wings and waded deep into the sand until my energy was spent; then lay panting in my enormous playpen.

Omar disappeared with a rope in his hand. Later, I saw him clear across many dunes hooking tree branches with his rope, tearing them down. Youssef had told him to get firewood. He wanted to show us how to make bread with hot sand. Omar went back and forth until a big pile of scraggy sticks heaped in front of us.

Omar stretched out on the sleeping mat.

"Ken, can you give me a massage? My back is tired."

Ken knelt beside Omar and worked on his back. He was meticulous, bending and stretching Omar's arms and legs one at a time.

"Ken, where did you learn this?" I asked.

"I used to do wrestling in school. We had to learn to take care of our teammates."

"Ken, can you use your feet? I can't feel anything," Omar whined loudly.

Ken stepped slowly onto Omar; with arms up, his feet inched across Omar's back. Now Omar was satisfied.

*

The fire leapt with a mighty roar as the branches crackled and sizzled. We kept feeding it. Excitement grew as the fire turned brazen, reddening our cheeks and foreheads. We had plenty of fuel. Every time Omar threw a big chunk of wood into the flames, they fragmented, sending a shower of sparkles every which way. I thought of pilots flying over the Sahara. They would surely see this fire, and wonder what was being sacrificed.

We drank soup while waiting for the fire to die down. Youssef and Omar broke the burning branches into nuggets with a stick. They pushed the nuggets to the side, exposing the hot sand underneath. Omar had made a large amount of dough earlier. The dough was placed directly onto the sand, and then covered with the red hot nuggets. Youssef grabbed a handful of cold sand and sprinkled onto different parts of the surface now and then to regulate the "oven" temperature. He tapped on the bread often, listening for the hollow sound. When he was satisfied that it was done, he pulled out the big black round. Youssef used a knife to scrape the surface until all the soot was gone. He wiped the bread with a wet towel and announced that dinner is served.

*

Ken and Omar fell asleep in front of the fire. I sat with my journal open, unable to write. Youssef came out of the tent after putting pots and pans away, and walked up the sand dune. I asked if he was going to watch the moonrise.

"Come," he said. I closed my journal and followed him. He extended his hand to help me with the last steps. We sat on the slope. He was quiet. I lay down on my stomach on the incline and looked out into the darkness. Youssef did the same and gestured for my hands. Wordlessly he kneaded my palms and fingers gently, one at a time.

A cold breeze brushed across my face. I shuddered. Youssef offered to bring up a blanket but I didn't want to stay there anymore. Under the night sky he transformed once again from a playful and lighthearted desert guide into a suitor enamored with his Oriental charge. As we came down the dune, I thanked him for taking care of me in this journey. He reached up and planted two kisses on my cheek.

My jumbled thoughts refused to become language. Words came laboriously as my pen paused long on the blank page. Restlessness rose like waves, throbbing in my temples. The men were all asleep, but their immobile shapes induced an agitation that brought me to my feet. I wrapped myself in a heavy blanket and walked out of the camp. The night sky spread before me.

Moon,
I do not come to the desert for you,
yet you have been following me,
waiting for this moment.
Your shafts stretch and lengthen
swivel before my eyes:
listen,
listen...

The desert was alive. I heard footsteps running, pittter-patter, stopping close to my back. The unseen murmured. The breeze conjured up its own tune, chanted faintly. I was spellbound. My mind blurred. Time and space folded, and with it, my earthly presence.

I bowed low to the moon.

*

The moon gazed at me at a different angle each time I woke during the night. I went back to sleep until the pale fish-belly color appeared in the east. Dawn was breaking. I wrapped the yellow turban around me and walked, barefoot, up the dune. There was no wind. Up high I could see a saturation of red and gold in the sky but didn't know how long it would take for the sun to rise. Some parts of the dunes were very cold. I walked back and forth to keep my feet from freezing. Then the moment came when among the ribbons of color the golden sun with its blinding rays blazed out of the horizon. I looked to my right. Half the sky was a tranquil lapis edged with pink, not yet affected by the sun. The moon was bright and clear, almost teary. A flock of birds flew over my head. I could hear the low flapping sound of their wings beating the air. And then the words came, distinct and clear:

> *The moon is your mother.*
> *The sun is your father.*
> *The desert is your home.*

I sat down and listened.

There were many lives in the Sahara when it was lush and fertile. After it dried up, life forms had to make changes. In order to survive, many moved away. However, each time they moved farther from their origin, they had to give up a part of themselves in exchange for the distance.

You have gone far but now you are home. Your origin will not change even though your physical forms in lives before and after may be different.

Youssef's face surfaced in my mind.

He is your brother. His origin and yours are the same. Don't be afraid of his affection.

I felt light and happy, ran down the dune into the tent and sat close to Youssef, warming my feet with his blanket. There was a sense of ease and joy. Omar was making more bread, and coffee was ready.

Another Arabic word:

Kasbah — a fortress

A Day in Zagora

I writhed in an airless hotel room with a window the size of a shoe box. My nose was acutely aware of the stale air. My body baked on the warm sheets all night. The desert had cleansed my senses and freed my spirit. Confined inside the concrete walls and locked door, I felt like a prisoner upon my re-entry into civilization.

Ken had to leave early in the morning to go back to Spain, then on to Greece before heading home. I got up to say goodbye. He had turned out to be a perfect companion. We respected each other's space, came together for just the right amount of conversation, and were at ease with silence.

Youssef came briskly in at 9:30 and asked me to pack.

"I'll take you to a nice and cheap place to stay."

He had borrowed his brother's motorbike and motioned me on. We rode the bike with my luggage in front to Amezrou, a small village just outside of Zagora. There, Youssef showed me a campground. A garden with palm trees and a gazebo provided a sense of tranquility—indeed a perfect place for respite.

After I checked in, we left for Youssef's house. He wanted me to meet his family.

Youssef's family lived on a hill in a basic three room mud house. When we arrived, his mother and grandmother were outside washing vegetables and preparing lunch. His sister-in-law had a baby on her back. While doing chores she watched two spunky children running about. The entrance to the house had no door panel and the windows no panes. The ground was dried mud. A long electrical cord from outside dangled through a crack on the wall and plugged into a television. It was positioned prominently in the main room. The only other fixture was a light bulb. Youssef showed me another room full of trunks and luggage. It contained the family's possessions. The third room was bare, used only for sleeping.

Youssef had to return the motorbike, so he left me with the women. His mother and sister-in-law brought out mats and cushions, and a small table for tea. My Arabic vocabulary soon ran out. I took out some gifts: a string of mini Tibetan prayer flags, stickers for the children, and some Chinese preserved plums wrapped individually in small packets. They brought out a plate of dates—a local delicacy. The fruits were so sugary they stuck on each other. When I pulled them the flesh came off the seeds like caramel.

One by one children's faces appeared in the doorway. Cousins and nephews returned from school to have lunch with the family. From a young age the boys learn to make tea and serve the adults. Before and after lunch a boy brought a metal bowl to each of us and poured water on our hands, and passed around soap and a towel.

Men and women sat around separate tables. A big shallow dish with a chimney-shaped lid was put on each table. Youssef's sister-in-law gave everyone flat bread. We dipped the bread into the dish and used it to scoop up the peas, carrots and potatoes. A piece of meat was at the bottom of the dish. Youssef's sister-in-law broke up the meat with her fingers and gave a portion to everyone.

After lunch, Youssef's mother motioned me to lie down beside her. She covered her head with a cotton scarf. I placed the yellow turban over my face and body. Although the room was clean and dry, flies were everywhere. The men went to sleep, lying on the opposite side of the room.

Youssef's sister-in-law put her baby down beside me and covered him with a translucent white cloth. She patted baby lightly until he fell asleep, then got up and left the room.

Soon Youssef's mother was snoring. I turned and looked at the small bundle next to me; black flies had rested like raisins atop a mound of vanilla pudding. The bundle stirred, and the flies would ascend and descend with its movements, as if they were choreographed. I could hear children playing outside and wondered if it would be improper for me to rise. After a while baby began to utter small cries. When they became more and more urgent, I lifted him up and cradled him in my arms. Flies buzzed around baby's big teary eyes; I had to keep fanning them out. Baby was just quieting down when his mother walked into the room. He let out a big wail, accusing her of absence, stretching out his little hands toward her. I was promptly relieved from duty.

*

In the late afternoon Youssef and I strode down a dirt road into an oasis full of palm trees. We walked to a village. The inhabitants seemed to be the poorest of the poor. Men and women sat in the dirt outside of their houses and stared without expression. Children quickly gathered around me asking, "One dirham, one dirham." Youssef chided them and they went on to something else.

To our right was a set of steps. This led to the kasbah of the Jews, a walled residential quarter with dark, tunnel-like passages. Gradual migration started after the establishment of the state of Israel, and the last Jewish family moved away in 1967. Now poor people lived here without water and electricity. Several boys were playing with stones and sling shots at the entrance. Youssef called out to them before we entered so we wouldn't get hit. Then he took my hand and led me through the ancient, winding, uneven mud path. With the walls high on each side and a slice of sky above, I heard only the soft crunching sound under our feet.

Youssef asked if I would stay a few more days.
"Maybe we can go to Marrakech together. I have to visit

my brother there, but it would have to be three days from now. If you stay, I will refuse work in the meantime."

"Youssef, I don't want you to stop working because of me. I like to travel alone, but it would be really nice to spend a last night at D'jamaa Elfna Square, if you can make it to Marrakech before I leave for America."

*

The next morning he came to my tent. I was still in bed writing, and motioned him to sit down beside me. He told me he was called to work and had to leave for the desert now.

"Go. You must go to work."

I gave him my hotel address in Marrakech. He put it in his shirt pocket. We gave each other a deep, long hug. He kissed my face tenderly. His hand slowly touched my hair, neck, and down toward my chest. I cupped it before it went any further. He lowered his eyes, hiding a mixture of longing and disappointment.

Youssef pulled out a photograph and handed it to me. It was a very good picture of him in a Berber outfit, sitting beside a camel.

"Remember me…you will come back?"

He stood up. I felt the distance lengthen between us as he spoke with a hearty voice, "Good luck. Good travel. Be safe!"

End of a Journey

The thought of Youssef weaved in and out of my mind. Did I reciprocate his affection? Perhaps Youssef was the spirit of Sahara reaching out, embracing its long-lost daughter. The gift of love was bestowed upon me. I knew in my heart the journey was completed.

The next morning, a shopkeeper pointed me in the direction of the parking lot, where grand taxis congregate to transport passengers to different cities.

"Go to Quarzazate first," he told me, "then transfer to another taxi to Marrakech."

Grand Taxi was a misnomer for these beat-up Mercedes sedans from a bygone era. A taxi would leave when it had six passengers. From Zagora to Quarzazate I sat in the back with two men and a large Berber woman. As the second person to enter the taxi, I was able to lean all the way to the back of the seat. The remaining space was tight. We wedged together like four ill fitted pieces to a jigsaw puzzle. The man next to me sat on the edge of the seat the whole way. He moaned once in a while, but there was silent agreement among us that any movement would cause more pain than comfort. The ride took three hours.

When we got off at Quarzazate, there was a taxi leaving for Marrakech right away. This time I had the misfortune of sitting in the front between the driver and another man. The man, though not big, fell asleep after a while. Once relaxed, he expanded. I found myself practically sitting on the driver's stick shift.

"No matter," the driver gestured. He was probably used to the situation. I, on the other hand, squeezed my thigh as much to the right as I could every time he shifted gears, which was often. Several times the gear wouldn't engage because my thigh was blocking it. I had to push myself up and slam heavily against the sleeping man. He seemed oblivious. The road snaked up and down the Atlas Mountains. We tumbled left and right.

After two hours we arrived at a block-long business strip. Our driver parked the taxi in front of a raised foundation. It was about the height of a one storey building, with a restaurant situated on top. Across the street there was a similar structure. On the edge of the foundations a line of tagine simmered on coals. It was a windy day. Thick gray smoke from the stews rolled down to the street below and picked up the yellow sand. They swirled a fierce dance and the sand flung repeatedly onto windshields and into people's faces. I wrapped my head and covered my face with the yellow turban and walked up to the restaurant. After ordering tea and an egg sandwich, I sat down at an outside table next to a meat stall. There was no smoke, sand, or wind where I sat. Watching taxis pulling in and out of the parking spaces, honking for dawdling passengers, I realized the high foundations were built with a purpose to provide shelters from the calamity below.

Chunks of beef, lamb, and organs were placed directly on the meat stall's tile counter. Half a lamb's body hung from a rod. A woman emerged from a taxi and went to the counter. She asked for ground meat. The butcher used a hand grinder and put her order on a piece of paper. The woman carried the lump of meat openly and returned to the taxi.

I was grateful there was no meat or livestock in my taxi. My neighbor suddenly seemed tolerable. I took out some cookies and passed them around. After another two hours of the same maneuver; we parted without a word of goodbye.

*

Back in Marrakech, I found myself longing for the Sahara. The music, voices, and the hectic crisscrossing of people in D'jamaa Elfna were now an energetic party without a soul. I looked to the sky. The sun and moon seemed aloof. I felt withdrawn, and at a deeper level brimmed with sadness.

I did not see Youssef again. Alone in my room, memories of our charmed interlude haunted me. During the night when someone knocked loudly on the hotel door, I wondered if it was he, and whether our encounter would have further meaning beyond the Sahara. Dryness developed in my throat. Exhaustion took over. I spent my last day sleeping. The yellow turban bunched up beside me. It smelled of sweat and cigarette ashes. In the morning, tiny grains of golden sand dusted the bed linen.

October 2008

Back again after one and a half years, I spent a week in Marrakech, venturing into the *Mellah*, an enclosed Jewish settlement; and Setti Fatma, a village in the Atlas Mountains. Dore joined me in the second week. Our story (*A Conversation with Murat*) began in Essouira, a seaside town on the Atlantic Ocean. We traveled southeast into the Anti-Atlas (part of the Atlas Mountains in the southwest region of Morocco), and the Sahara Desert. We then turned north to Tangier, crossing the Strait of Gibraltar into Spain.

Another Arabic word:
Mellah — an enclosed Jewish settlement

Touch

The hand was on my shoulder when bargaining, at my elbow when someone wanted to pass me, and sometimes a pat in the back to warn of motorbike cruising down a narrow street. Men held hands, hugged and punched each other like children at play. Women too, they walked arm in arm in the streets. I flared up the first time a shop keeper tried to lure me into his shop by holding my arm. He backed off, surprised at my reaction. Of course I had to be careful of those stealthy hands that touched me in the back inappropriately, sliding their fingers down my buttocks. That usually happened at night in D'jemaa Elfna and it was hard to catch these sleazy intruders. They melted expertly into the crowd. In any case, my sense of touch was heightened at hands that were moving, stretching, waving and fingers that were pointing, snapping, knitting themselves into the everyday fabric of life.

*

On the edge of the Mellah a woman shop keeper eyed me casually as I approached. She didn't say anything like "big welcome" or "where you from." What was I looking for? A d'jellaba. She had many hanging high in a row in her shop. I studied each of them carefully.

"Would you like to try on this one?" She pointed at a dark blue d'jellaba.

"...no, I don't think I like any of them," I said, disappointed because I would like to buy something from her. I had never seen a woman working in a shop before. Was she the only one?

"I'm the only one in the Mellah. There are other women running their shops in the souk."

She was wearing an ash pink headscarf and a reddish brown d'jellaba with tiny threads of red, yellow and green stitched into the fabric, subtle, understated and elegant.

"I like your d'jellaba," I said admiringly.

"You like? Really?"

"Yes. I would like a d'jellaba like this one."

Her nose wrinkled a little and her eyes turned mischievous. Stepping quickly to the front of the shop she took out a long stick. She put it across the width of the shop with the ends resting on the top part of the shelves on both sides. Now she took out two huge scarves and draped them over the stick, transforming the shop into a changing room.

"Just for fun," she said, taking off her d'jellaba. She gave it a good kiss and handed it to me. I put it on. My body was much smaller. The d'jellaba fell on me shapelessly.

"You look better in it than me." I told her.

She was wearing a white turtle neck and black pants under the d'jellaba but without it she felt naked. She quickly took down the dark blue d'jellaba and put it on. Now we were giggling at each other. She pushed me forward to look into a mirror. Mmmm, not as bad as I thought...

"...I give you good discount. Support your sister."

She rolled her d'jellaba into a bundle after we agreed on the price.

*

The Mellah was an area populated by the Jews five hundred years ago. Now it was mainly a spice market. It seemed very poor people lived here in this enclosed area. Children flocked around me asking for money and pointing the way to the synagogue. The synagogue hid behind a set of rust-colored metal doors. A long corridor led into a blue tiled courtyard. Pictures of past rabbis were hung on the walls. The synagogue served additionally as a shelter for homeless women and children. The rabbi, toothless and with a wispy crown of snow white hair looked ancient, but managed to unlock the temple for us. Inside, rows of green and gold brocade armchairs lined three sides of the room and down the middle. The altar was covered by a gigantic curtain embroidered with the tablets. A balcony in the back was the section for women.

The Jewish cemetery was several bends away from the synagogue, surrounded by a red wall. The gate keeper came forward as we entered.

"Are you Jewish?" Dore asked him.

"No. Muslim. Doesn't matter, Jews, Muslims, Christians. No problem, no problem."

The cemetery was the size of a football field. Low lying grave stones, pale from age, filled the area like oblong pillboxes or lipstick cases. These graves were made of red bricks and poured over with cement. Between the graves the ground was also filled with cement. Dry grass and weeds sprout in the cracks. There was no path.

"The middle section is for children and the nameless. The section on the right is for the women, and the section to the left is for the men."

"Why nameless? Why didn't they have names?"

He couldn't tell us.

The gate keeper pointed out several bigger graves at the entrance, isolated from the rest. Those were the rabbis' graves.

The afternoon sun brought out the starkness of disrepair as we walked around the ones without names and stepped over some that were dilapidated with the cement half gone, and the bricks coming apart underneath. Only two hundred and fifty Jews lived in Marrakech nowadays.

Big yellow dogs ran about the cemetery. They were the living inhabitants in this desolate flat land. As we went deeper, we saw names on many of the graves. Some graves have the evidence of being visited. They have small pieces of stones on them. I put a stone on one of the graves, touching someone unknown.

Milude

Setti Fatma was a Berber village in the Atlas Mountains. To get there from Marrakech I had to take a grand taxi. A grand taxi would leave the station when it had six passengers. It was early afternoon when I arrived at the station. This must be the slow time of the day because there were no passengers waiting to go anywhere. Only the taxi drivers were milling around.

"It'll cost you 250 dirhams to Setti Fatma," a man swaggered over to me.

"No. I want to go in a collective."

The man walked me to a taxi. The driver waiting there smiled at me shyly, took my luggage and put it in his trunk. He had a head full of black hair and a matching thick moustache so that his head looked out of proportion from his slim body.

"How much does it cost to go in a collective?" I asked him. He didn't speak much English, but we managed to figure out about 25 dirhams per person.

"OK. I'll wait."

We waited. For twenty minutes there was not a single request. The man who asked for 250 dirhams spoke a bit more English. He told me they would not go unless there were six people. However I could pay 150 dirhams and go now.

I hired the grand taxi.

The taxi driver opened the back door for me.
"May I sit in the front?" I asked.

We drove down a straight highway and immediately we were away from the hustle and bustle of Marrakech.
"What's your name?" I asked the driver in Arabic.
"My name is Omar."

Omar was pleasantly surprised that I spoke his language,

and so was I, after not speaking it for over a year. We spoke, in broken English and Arabic about our lives, and listened to Arabic and Berber music from his cassettes.

"Not so many tourists come here," I observed as the taxi wound uphill, passing small villages.

One car came down on the other side and passed us.
"Ah! Tourists." I pointed at the people in the car.
He laughed. " You no tourist. You Berber."

When we arrived at Setti Fatma it was already around 3pm. Omar left me in front of the last hotel in the village. A lady with dyed blond hair and black high heel boots showed me the room. It had only a bed in it but the window looked out to the big stream running alongside the road. The toilet was in the hallway—the squat type— and if I wanted to take a shower I would have to ask for hot water.

The lady was eating lunch with two other women while I was filling in the registration. They invited me to sit down and eat with them, and offered me a plate of spicy fried fish, a bowl of stewed beans and lots of bread to mop up the juice.

The weather was at least twenty degrees colder in the Atlas than in Marrakech. Setti Fatma and many of the Berber villages were situated on each side of the terraced mountains. A wide stream ran between them. Crude-looking suspension bridges connected the two sides.

I took a walk after lunch. The stream was dry at this time of the year. Water level had shrunk to running in the middle, exposing large areas of rocks, pebbles and sand. People wandered in the dry area. Smoke billowed as a group of girls baked mud balls, using charcoal bits and a worn meshed grill. On the hillside a man pulled a donkey with a child sitting on it. They slowly walked toward the water. A few men on the other side of the stream were splitting woods and making a bridge.

The mountain passes trapped the clouds. When the gray was fully saturated it began to rain. I walked past a restaurant. Someone inside waved at me enthusiastically. A couple of tagines were cooking on pots of coal on a table under the veranda. I went over. The man came forward and shook my hand.

"Welcome, I am Berber." His flattened facial features were warm and congenial.

"Thank you, I am Chinese."

Two boys were watching some music videos on a small machine. One was the man's son, Jamal, and the other his friend. I asked the boys about trekking and seeing the waterfalls. The boy who was the friend said he could take me. He was no more than fifteen years old, with blushed cheeks, and his tight cropped hair had little curls brushed upward on his forehead. His voice was not high but I don't think it had broken yet, and so it retained a soft and gentle quality. There were many men in the street soliciting business. But I would prefer this boy who spoke Berber, French and Arabic but very little English.

"How much?"

"Two hundred dirhams."

"I don't want to spend that much." This was a bargain culture. Besides he was just a child.

"One hundred dirhams," he offered.

I accepted.

Like a gentleman he walked me back to my hotel after I finished a cup of coffee.

"What's your name?"

"Milude."

"Why don't you have school tomorrow?"

"My father, dead." He put his hands together and lay them on one side of his cheeks.

Back in the hotel room I searched my guide book. It said average guide fee in Setti Fatma should be around 250 dirhams.

All night I listened to the rushing of water.

Next morning Milude came to the hotel. We crossed the footbridge that was lain down by the men yesterday. The planks were not even tied down. We went up the stony pass, me climbing, sometimes on all fours and him walking with his hands in his pockets, except when he had to pull me up.

"Milude, I'm an old lady," I heaved.

"No, no," he patted on a rock for me to sit down, "After this we go my house. Meet mother. She makes couscous. Yes?"

The waterfalls tumbled down the rocky hillsides into pools. Four men came behind us, two Berbers and their customers. "Milude," they nodded at him, while pushing the fat bottom of a man up an incline of loose stones. Once beside the pool they sat down, took pictures and ordered drinks. Perhaps that was as far as they could go. Quiet descended as we moved away from the water and I found myself surrounded by the folds of the Atlas. The sun had chased away the morning rain and the sky became a brilliant blue. I opened my backpack and took out a bag of candy.

"Milude, this is for you."

"Thank you."

"Open it. You can have some now."

He weighed the bag in his hand and gave it back to me.

"Give it to mother." He said, smiling. "Gift."

Two Berber women and their floppy-ear goats came down from a hidden path. Each had a big basket full of hay tied to their backs. "Milude," they greeted him. We followed them downhill.

"Milude," shouted some young urchins playing in the street, looking at me with lopsided smiles.

"Milude," an old man kindly patted him on his shoulder.

Milude led the way, walking steadily with hands in pockets, into a carpet shop.

"Sit down, sit down. We'll make tea." The salesman had just gone out. Would we have tea and wait for a few minutes?

"Milude, I have no intention of buying carpets. I don't want to waste their time."

He understood. We thanked the man in the shop and walked out.

And uphill again, walking across bare mountain on the side of Setti Fatma, beside pipelines that bring water up to the houses. Villagers' footsteps stamped out the paths. Houses were built here and there without any order. Milude's house was in the middle of the hill, a concrete house with a small courtyard.

A toddler ran up to Milude as he entered the house. A young girl was washing dishes in the courtyard. She wore a long blue-jean skirt that accentuated her slim figure. Her long curly hair was tied in the back.

"My sister Suaad." She came over and we patted cheeks.

Milude's mother is a heavyset Berber woman. Her hair was hidden in a black scarf that twisted around her head. I can see youth in her eyes but she is a widow who must depend on her son. When I came into the kitchen she was separating couscous with her fingers on a large plate. Simmering on the stove was a big pot of carrot, turnip and chicken stew.

"How many children do you have?" I asked her in Arabic, sitting on a low stool.

"Three. Fatima is married. Milude is the middle one, and Suaad is the youngest. The baby is Fatima's son. We take care of him for her." She counted with her fingers cheerfully, then asked Milude to show me the living room.

Long cushions in blue and gold brocade materials lined three sides of the room. The floor was carpeted. A television set in one corner, and a small table beside a window that looked out into the backyard, where a few chickens were pecking away. Milude pulled out a photo album from a box.

"Father." He pointed to a magnificent Berber with deep set eyes and firm nose and mouth. He stood tall among his customers. There were group shots of ten or twelve people. Some of the pictures were taken in this living room. After trekking in the mountains he brought his customers home for meals.

Life must have been good then, with mother constantly cooking for new friends from all over the world, and Milude went on some of these expeditions with his father.
"Your son is a very good guide," I told her as we lunched. "Milude knows the mountains well."

She was pleased, kneading the couscous with her hand into a half ball and pushed a small piece of chicken on it with her thumb.

I hugged her on my way out, and pressed a couple of bills into her hand. Her young eyes shone, and she held me again in a tight embrace.
"Take care of yourself," I whispered. Perhaps I was saying it to myself. I felt a tinge of tightness in my nose.

We walked passed a mosque in the middle of the hill. Service had just ended, and villagers poured out of the building. They stepped on the loose stones briskly, sliding past me on my left and right. Milude waited for me at the bottom of the hill. He walked me back to the hotel.
"You rest. I wait here. Then we go Berber villages."

I washed up and went downstairs to meet him. He was sitting outside with the lady who gave me lunch yesterday.
"See waterfalls?"
"Yes. Milude was a good guide."
"What else can he do?" She shrugged her shoulders and opened her hands as she asked the question, shaking her head.

She gave Milude a glass of coke. They all knew the fatherless boy. Their sympathy was apparent.

Yet Milude carried himself with a quiet dignity. The men who were pestering me for business the day before had left us alone.

*

At a distance the suspension bridges that strung across the river looked like flimsy cloth lines. We sat on the side of the road and watched two villagers walk across the bridge with baskets on their backs.

"I want to cross over to the other side," I told Milude.

There was hesitation on his face but he couldn't explain it to me.

"Just cross over, and then we'll come back," I assured him.

We walked down a steep slope until we reached the bridge. It was made of twisted cables. The ends were cemented on the ground. I stepped on the wooden planks. The bridge began to sway. After a few steps it was moving up and down so violently I had to stop. The water underneath was in full force here, churning up white foams as it rushed downstream. As we approached the other side, a few heads popped out of the windows of the village houses. A man walked down close to the bridge and spoke to Milude. He didn't seem welcoming. Perhaps they did not want tourists here.

Walking back, Milude asked me if I knew how much would a motorcycle cost.

"You want one? I don't know, maybe forty thousand dirhams." I figured five thousand U.S. Dollars was probably right.

"Forty thousand! Really?" He looked disappointed.

"Don't believe me. What do I know about motorcycles!"

It was around five in the afternoon when we arrived at the restaurant where we met the day before. The man came out and asked me if I had a good day.

"I knew his father very well. We were good friends," his small eyes glistened.

I ordered his Berber tagine and invited Milude to have dinner with me. His friend Jamal now served as waiter.

In front of the hotel I pulled out a bill. Two hundred dirhams, as Milude had suggested initially. He thanked me happily, and wished me "Bon Voyage," then turned and walked down the semi-darkened street, his hands in his pockets, unhurried.

Babouche Impromptu

I'm wearing the pointy toed, fuchsia pink, soft leather Moroccan slippers and feeling the rush to D'jamaa Elfna. Mohammad standing next to rows of colors: eggplant, pomegranate, indigo, grasshopper, egg yolk, orange and walnut looked rather dull in comparison to his line of merchandise. He is the bee working for the flowers, getting tourists like me to salivate over the rainbow selection, feeling the soft goat skin, marveling at the inlaid, where at the end of it all his pot of gold may be plenished.

How much of "the gold" goes into his pocket, and how much goes to the bland-faced workers in Mohammad's little one room factory next door? Maybe they are his family, you know, uncles, nephews, aunts who can't speak English but have been making babouches since the beginning of time. They work under a couple of dangling light bulbs, punching holes and hand stitching the slippers, surrounded by the pungent smell. It's not from the leather, but the dye that soaks the skins, turning them into brilliant colors. Put the slippers close to your nose and you'd puke. Imagine the tannery where cow urine and pigeon droppings are the main ingredients. How much is a pair of babouches? Less than ten dollars. Mohammad with his white cotton shirt and black pants is immaculate and patient, explaining the different styles: round toed Berber, pointy-toed Moroccan and curly-toed Aladdin. I giggled. Oh yes, I can see myself in this and in that. Rubber bottom for outdoor and leather ones for indoor. I want to take them all with me, Mohammad.

Men and women in d'jellabas shuffle in babouches around Marrakech all day. Their exposed heels blackened with dirt, and the sheath-like slippers caked with mud look nothing like the alluring ones on my feet. These lucky ones are going to be my play things on carpeted floor. They'll never see the sidewalk, let alone slippery and pebbled streets that snaked around the medina. When they get dirty I clean them with a wet towel.

Mohammad gives a dirham to a boy and he brings back a glass of mint tea. For you, he said. It's their culture to take care of strangers even if I don't buy anything from him. But in my head I calculate. He is depleting his pot so maybe I'm a big customer who he thinks will buy more than one pair. My western thinking allows me to divide and subdivide the profit he makes so he can pay himself, his rent, factory, his materials and workers; dividing the profit for the whole Moroccan economy—money Mohammad makes from me buying a pair of babouches!

The pleasure of money. You can see the chain of cause and effect so clearly in a mere dirham. The power you have when you're holding it, and the people who are affected by its portioning out when you let go. It's my goddess complex. Sometimes more obvious than others, but I have it over the babouches.

More Arabic Words:

seen — China
"hairdee mez'yana b'sef" — "this is very good"
shoui-a — a little
wahid, joush, thelata — one, two, three
"Shukran and bislema" — "thank you and good bye"

A Conversation with Murat

"Too many French tourists in Essouira," Dore complains as we sit in a neighborhood restaurant just outside of the city. He is speaking to a local man who has left his friends to check out the strangers.

"What about you? You tourists."

"We're travelers."

"Ah yes. Big welcome!" The man nods as if he really understands the difference.

"I learn English three years." He points to another man sitting at the next table. "That's my teacher. He knows a lot. Hey professor, come over," he motions his arm in big circles.

The professor smiles and raises his cigarette hand. Smoke billows between his index and middle finger. He'll wait.

"Big welcome. Big welcome," he turns back. " Where you from?"

"San Francisco. The United States."

"No," he leans his body closer to the table. " Where you from, origin?"

"I'm from Hong Kong, China."

"Ahhh, *Seen*." He sits back, satisfied.

"Big welcome. I live here. This my street. It's a good street. Good street, yes?"

"Yes," I agree, smiling at his enthusiasm.

He is laughing now. His upper teeth are all gone. His gum looks grayish. As he laughs, saliva drips from his mouth. He wipes it with the back of his hand. His fingers long and slender, dirty nails.

"I live there," he points vaguely down the street. "Every day I see my friends. This is good street, best street."

Dore takes out his camera. He watches him, one arm on the table.

"May I take your picture?"

He straightens up; his right index finger wagging in front of him, his head turning slowly from side to side.

"No."

"Why not?"

"I'm not ... strange thing you bring back America."

He is not angry but sincerely trying to explain his reasoning, "What we take you picture when we come in America. What you feel?"

"I want a picture of you so I can remember our friends in Morocco, but it's fine if you don't want your picture taken." Dore puts the camera away.

"No, no, we're not...exotique!" His head leans back; his cigarette fingers draw an invisible line in the air.

"That's not my intention at all."

"Why I come sit here? I am welcome you. Just be friends. Hospitality. Just be friends." His earnestness intensifies.

"I understand your reasoning and I do respect your point of view," I try to calm him.

"Ahhh...no problem, no problem," he softens, muttering to himself. His eyes are a little red on his milk-chocolate, clean shaven face. If he had all his teeth he could be a handsome man.

The professor comes over with a plastic bag in his hand. He opens it and takes out two steaming hot layered pancakes.

"Eat, eat," he speaks through his thick mustache.

"Thank you. Please eat with us. We're waiting for our harira soup."

"It'll come," he assures us, "they bring from another place."

We tug at the pancakes. The layers come apart, soft and delicious.

"Eat, eat," I gesture. "*Hairdee mez'yana b'sef.* I have not seen this kind of pancake anywhere in the medina."

"This make here. Down the street. Good eh?" They are very pleased.

"You speak Arabic?" He asks me.
"*Shoui-a.*"
"*Shoui-a* is good. You have children?"
"Two. I have one son and one daughter," I reply in Arabic.
"Ah good. Can you count to ten?"

But they also want to count. So we all count in unison: *wahid, joush, thelata...*, clapping our hands at the end, roaring with laughter.

It's time to introduce ourselves.
"What's your name?"
    "Murat."

The professor's name is Hassan. He speaks even less English and he seems restless, sliding his hand down Dore's arm and grins, winking. At the same time his head does a slow rotation so that his chin moves toward his shoulder and up, leaning at an angle. His eyes turn glassy.

The harira soup finally arrives. They light up their cigarettes and let us drink in silence.
Murat gets up. "I go buy another pancake for you."

He leaves before I can stop him.

We repeat the conversation with the professor: where we're from, good neighborhood, good food, good Essouira. Murat comes back and puts a pancake on the plate.

Dore takes out his camera and starts taking pictures of me. He shows them.
"Ah, *mez'yana, mez'yana.*"

Dore asks the professor," May I take your picture?"

Murat shakes his head at the professor, but the professor is happy to pose. They exchange a few words in Arabic. There is tightness in Murat's face but he soon relaxes and looks at the pictures in the camera with us.

"When you leave?"

"We're leaving tomorrow night."

"When you come next time you stay here. I find you good place."

"Yes. I'll come to this street and ask for Murat."

"Yes yes yes," his mouth dripping, his long arms flinging on his sides. "You ask for me. Everyone knows me here."

They walk back to their friends' table when we pay our bill. We go over to say goodbye.

"*Shukran wu bislema.*" I shake Murat's hand. He pulls me forward and presses his lips on my cheeks.

The sky is dark and an orange moon is rising as we walk back to our hotel. I drift slowly into a pensive mood.

"Dore, if someone stops you in San Francisco and asks to take your picture so he can show his friends what an American looks like, what would you do?"

"They can take my picture."

"So you'll represent all Americans?"

"Well?" He turns to me, bookish, bald, slim and Jewish.

Night Ride

The pains in my neck and back and the bus' grinding change of gear woke me often. Confined on a synthetic fabricated seat, my buttocks suffered uncomfortably from a dull heat that was self generated. My legs stretched forward under the seat in front. Next to me, Dore had to keep his knees apart to fit in the narrow seat. Two o'clock in the morning and we were winding our way from the Atlantic coast into the Anti-Atlas Mountains. Fog washed the air, blurring trees and shrubs as if they were ink smudges on rice paper. Yet the bus driver curved one hairpin turn after another.

Most passengers had left the bus at Agadir, a big modern seaside tourist resort. Our destination was Tafraoute, a town deep in the Anti-Atlas. It would take ten hours to get there.

The bus stopped, abruptly, woke me again from my stupor. I saw out of the yellow headlights hooded and robed figures stepping onto the bus. *Where are we?* Not town, not village, nor bus station. These men appeared out of nowhere. They had been waiting along the mountain highway.

The pointed tips of grey, blue and black hoods looked mysterious in the diffused light, but in fact they were just ordinary village workers trying to get home. The one sitting across from us retched, straining and gagging loudly until he vomited into a black plastic bag handed to him when he got on the bus. The Berbers could ride on donkeys or walk for hours but they had a long way to go getting used to riding in vehicles.

The sky began to brighten. All the hooded passengers got off at a village. A roadside cafe had a steaming white (milk or almond?) soup waiting for them. The men shook hands with each other, lighted cigarettes and poured mint tea.

I could see the landscape now, rolling hills dotted with

trees. Up and down mountain roads, rectangular minarets were the markers of villages. A group of young Berber girls appeared from around a bend. They were covered from top to bottom in black, but the trims were colorful with embroidery or sequins, zigzagging down one side of their bodics. Each one held a part of her veil and brought it over the nose, but I could see a dark eye, or an exquisite contour of a face, or a peek of lips. Like morning birds they chirped, rousing the sleepers, welcoming the sun.

One more Arabic word:
haloof — pig

The Forbidden Fruit

Sheets of red and purple granite jabbed at the blue sky. The Ameln villages were strung along the foothills. From a distance the houses looked like they were carved out of the cliffs. We entered the first village from the highway, walking past palm groves, cacti, almond, olive and argan trees; and desert flowers blossoming in lilac and crimson hues. Water troughs and pipelines fertilized the vegetation. A plastic cup tied on a long string dangled from a trough. The sparkling mountain water was for all to drink.

Climbing to the cliff dwellings, looking in through partial walls and stepping on crumbling bricks and stones, we realized most of them were ruins. Cement houses painted in rose color were inhabited by people, but we saw few villagers after an hour of wandering.

The sun poured its late morning rays through the leaves of a jade green tree, warming the blue and white metal doors, softly baking a high wall of mud and stones. A man came down the dirt path with his little girl on a donkey. She wore a pair of large round rim glasses, magnifying her eyes.

A Shepherd leaned on a rock watching his black and brown goats climbing up and down, nibbling at an argan tree. An old man sat in the back of his house shelling argan nuts with a heavy rock. They smiled their leather-face smiles. Deep-set eyes that could see for miles, pink tongues hidden behind a few smoke-stained teeth, horny fingernails and toenails, their dark-brewed coffee skin wrinkled like the trunk of the argan tree. Timeless men. The Anti-Atlas toughened and twisted their forms in its bowels until they became unmistakably part of the land-scape.

A group of young boys wrestling in the clearing away from the houses broke the tranquility of our walk. They kicked

up a dust storm, threw each other on the pebbled ground,
punching the opponents' heads and stomachs. They looked about
eight to nine years old. Their backpacks were thrown under
a big tree. Surely nothing was better than a good fight after
school. They were imitating Jackie Chan, the famous Chinese
kungfu movie star. When they saw me they wondered if I knew
kungfu. Then the boys decided that following the foreigners might
be more interesting than fighting.

"I love you madam," the boys shouted, pushing each
other hard so one of them fell against me. They giggled. Trailing
behind Dore, a boy offered me some dark purple berries. His
eyes widened, his mouth O-shaped and he kept gesturing his
hand to his mouth. I ate one—dry and chewy—and spitted the
little seed out like the boy.
"Where do these berries come from?" I gestured.

They pointed down. The berries were lying in rock crev-
ices and the muddy ground near a bush.
"What is the name of the berry?" I asked them, just in
case if I get sick I would be able to tell people what I had swallowed.
"*Esgour*," they said, shoving the berries into their mouths.
"*Haloof*," one boy said to another.
"What! Pig eats this?"
"No no," they laughed.

We walked to a general store. Its front door was
blocked by a high counter and the shop keeper looked out as we
approached. Standing in front of the counter the boys took out
their money to buy candy. One of them offered his to me. They
were all rowdy shouting over each other when suddenly they
froze. I turned around. An elderly man in d'jellaba stood a short
distance down the path with his hands spread out.
"Mohammad," he called out sternly. One of the boys
walked obediently towards him.
"That's Mohammad's father," the boys told me after they
were gone.

Shop keeper Brahim carried a basket of bread and sodas and bolted up his shop. We all walked up the village together. When we came to a house he took out a large bottle of orange soda and asked one of the boys to knock on the door. After a few minutes an old lady peeked out and took the bottle. We continued uphill to a house where Brahim delivered the bread and the lady of the house made us coffee and tea. It was time to say goodbye to the boys. I took out a bag of candy and gave each of them a few, and told them to save some for Mohammad.

As Dore and I walked out of the village, big green cacti with fleshy leaves the shape of tennis rackets dominated the landscape. Their oval shaped red fruits looked like swollen toes on top of green palms. We had this fruit in Marrakech, 5 dirhams apiece, peeled and cut for us. Here they were in abundance, growing wild. The fruits had sharp black thorns on the skins, but I saw some that had none and reached up and squeezed one. It felt plump and ready. I twisted it out of the leaf. The top opened, revealing the semi-translucent flesh, crimson and oozing juice. I pulled the skin down and quickly felt my fingers stung by tiny hair-like spikes that were invisible to me. Too late now. I peeled the whole fruit and ate it, slurping the sweet nectar and swallowing the pearl-like seeds.

The next hour was spent picking the spikes out of my fingers. No wonder the vendors who sold this fruit wore gloves, children didn't pick them and birds didn't bother. But I had eaten the forbidden fruit, with nectar drip-dried on my face. I licked the corner of my mouth and felt no shame.

I'brahim and Aisha

I'brahim and Aisha went into the Chigaga region of the Sahara Desert with Youssef and two camels. Two days before, it had rained. The sandy floor had turned into a mud plain. The sun baked the earth into clay and the thin brittle surfaces cracked under their feet. Youssef in his black turban, light blue long tunic with gold nomadic emblem walked in a relaxed manner, leading the camels on a leash. He told I'brahim and Aisha to walk in the camels' shadows so they wouldn't be scorched by the sun. I'brahim put on a dark blue turban, the color of nomads'. It covered his head and face, exposing only his large eyeglasses. Aisha draped her head with a yellow turban, the color of the sun. She trailed behind her companions with her dainty steps.

Hours and hours they walked, crossing deserts of black and blue stones, crossing dry riverbeds covered in small shrubs and fossil rocks, crossing rippling sand dunes. Youssef made lunch under an Acacia tree: a Berber salad of tomatoes, onions, green peppers and cucumbers with sardine; and a pot of cumin chicken with plenty of sauce. I'brahim and Aisha rested on long mats in the shadow of the tree and drank strong sugary green tea. They were too tired to move. While they napped, Youssef washed all the dishes and packed them away.

On and on they walked. Aisha's delicate ankles began to hurt. She didn't complain but Youssef wisely put her on the camel. Aisha could see from the hump the camel's small fuzzy brown ears sticking out. His long neck curved downward and up, rotating at the end as his powerful thighs moved back and forth.

At night they made camp on the sand. Aisha and I'brahim gathered dried sticks and made a small fire. Youssef sang and played drum on a large green water can.

"Dance, Aisha!" He commanded.

Aisha, barefoot in her white d'jellaba with black thin

stripes got up and danced, clapping her hands to the drum beat, lifting her head to the stars. I'brahim pulled out his mini recorder and stopped the show.

"Ok. Start again," he said after he pushed the "record" button.

That night Aisha saw the moon three times, each at a different angle as she slept and woke. I'brahim woke to the gurgling sounds of the camels and found them sitting in the sand, facing each other, rubbing necks.

Youssef opened his eyes as soon as he heard Aisha stirring beside him. He got up and started to boil water for tea and coffee. There were bread and jam and soft cheese for breakfast, peppered with a little sand.

The sky was bright blue, and the sun rose rapidly. After swishing Listerine in his mouth, I'brahim took off his clothes. His skin was pale as the dawning sand. He changed into a pure white long shirt down to his ankles. As he walked his white shirt shimmered against the dunes, now deepening into gold as the sun intensified. I'brahim's form fluttered in the breeze as he trailed behind Youssef. Aisha sitting high on the camel wound the turban on her head and covered her face. The sun impressed itself on her nose, turning it red. Her black hair felt wiry and sandy. She waved her hand in front of her eyes. Flies flew up and landed back on her yellow turban. From a distance I'brahim thought they looked like raisins.

They walked much of the day, stopping to make a Berber omelet with onions, tomatoes and cumin; and lots of strong tea. Aisha was most happy in the evening, after the grueling day, to sit on top the dune and gaze at the stars. She thought of her children and wrote their names on the sand. A shooting star brought her wishes to her faraway home.

They slept in a tent because it was cold and windy. Aisha slept between Youssef and I'brahim. Three bodies each covered under heavy and sandy blankets. She felt Youssef's restlessness, grunting and turning in the night.

On the last day Youssef took Aisha's hand and walked with her. Youssef's legs were lean and powerful. His feet were thick and every toe was muscular. Aisha counted; they were walking three paces to a second. Her breaths became heavy as she stumbled up the sand dunes. Youssef held her hand firmly, tugging her arm to his side. After a short time Aisha's throat was parched and she could hear her heartbeats in her ears. Youssef put her back on the camel.

I'brahim was delighted to find a herd of goats after they crossed the Zagora River. He walked with the shepherds until they arrived at M'hamid, their destination desert town. Aisha stood in a mud path between houses and watched the camels being unloaded. A few girls who were playing jump rope down the path ran over to Aisha. When she uncovered her face they kept staring at her. Aisha opened her backpack and took out a candy. She gave it to the girl nearest her. Suddenly many children ran out of the mud houses, their hands outstretched, circling around Aisha.

"Bon bon, bon bon," they cried.

After Aisha handed out all her candy, she went into a mud house with I'brahim and Youssef. There, friends awaited them and they had lunch together sitting on the carpeted floor around a low table. Before they left, I'brahim and Aisha gave Youssef big hugs and thanked the camels. They took off their turbans and resumed their former personas.

Threesome with Jack Kerouac

To think I'm in bed with him, and in the deep of night he turned and put his arms around me.

"You," he breathed, "you're a poet of exceptional quality. After tonight you'll write fiercely like me, write until your brain incinerates and your hands writhe."

Dore was a bit surprised when I wanted to change from the bigger room number 6 with bath and toilet to this corner room number 5 with no toilet.

"The window creaked open three times and so did the door. This room is haunted."

But I wanted it haunted. I wanted to be haunted by Jack Kerouac in room number 5 in the hotel El Muniria on Rue Magellan, where he stayed for weeks. His novel *Desolation Angels* might have been written here. At the Tangier train station none of the taxi drivers knew where the hotel was even when we gave them the map. Finally one guy took us there. From the main drag that looked like downtown Los Angeles he swiveled right at the corner of the Blue Bar, left onto a dark residential street and stopped at the dead end.

"El Muniria," he pointed up at the sign. Rue Magellan was a seedy-looking alley that had a short run downhill.

A black heavy iron door led to a narrow hallway and the reception cubbyhole. The red-haired woman tried to pacify a child and registered us at the same time.

"Cocktail hour starts at ten o'clock," she smiled.

But we were not drinkers, nor did we smoke. A generation from the Beatniks, I was more interested in their rooms— red doors, skeleton keys, and spider silks that might still vibrate with stories.

Jack must have left something behind. Hair, skin, cells,

smell could be trapped in the dusty corners. He might have spilled something inside the blue dresser. My bare feet shuffled on the sage green tiled floor: mine on his. The mildewed air, the heavy wood blinds, Jack's hands pulling the cord. A square table was covered with a cigarette-stained blue-checkered cloth. Two chairs and a glass ashtray—a smoke with Allen Ginsberg. The bed! Oh the mattress seemed too firm to be fifty years old. The sheets too fresh, the long pillow that ran across the width of the bed was white and puffed. The bathroom though, in the absence of a toilet, had a bidet. *THAT* was imaginable, Jack washing himself in this china basin, now dusty and grey.

William Burroughs wrote *Naked Lunch* in room number 9. The room was private now. Someone lived in it permanently. I held onto the wood banister and walked up the stairs. The door to the terrace was missing a chunk at the bottom. Rain water splattered in, making the landing wet. When I reached the top floor I saw the numbers 7 and 8 on the doors to my right. Room 9 was directly at the top of the stairs with its wall sticking partially out. The door was opened. I would get caught if I turned left and looked in. No further.

I slid into the covers and closed my eyes.

Jack?" I whispered.
"Yes?"
"What are you doing?"
"Writing a book."
"In the dark?"
"Of course."
"What's it about?"
"Mopeds and Beggars."

I laughed, leaned over and kissed his cheek.

Crossing the Continental Divide

Couldn't buy a cup of coffee with the Moroccan dirhams.
We were still in Morocco, or at least in its water at the Port of
Tangier. Perhaps it was because the piece of floating real estate
we had boarded belonged to some shipping corporation in Spain
or France. Their business with the Moroccans stopped at the
dock.

"Go downstairs to the little booth and they will change
dirhams into euros, then come back and get your coffee," said the
attendant.

The triple-level ferry had chrome railings, thick blue
commercial carpeting and dark green padded velour seats that
could accommodate hundreds. Picture windows lined the entire
ship. You couldn't miss the rock of Gibraltar. Television sets were
spaced throughout the two floors. They repeatedly announced
safety and emergency procedures in English, Spanish and
French. Moroccans must be able to understand any of the above
languages. Otherwise if the ferry capsized they would have no
help but Allah.

At the port, two men fought in the street while I was
waiting for Dore to purchase the ferry tickets. Men milled about
in front of the offices of different companies. They were there to
seize tourists' attention, show them the ferry's time schedule and
pricing. Maybe they receive a commission from the company.
Maybe they get a tip from the tourists. A tall man with a green
vest who looked semi-official counted some bills in his hand and
handed them off to another. Several men watched the transaction
in a semi-circle until a long-faced, skinny man started shouting.
It aggravated the man in green. He pushed the skinny man on his
shoulders and before long the man came back and punched him
under the chin. Someone tried to break up the fight and stood
between them. No good. They stalked each other like dogs. One
ran down the street and the other pursued. Now they stood a few
feet away from me, dark, dangerous, grunting fury. The lady at

the ticket sales window looked out in disgust.

"Uneducated men," her mouth curved downward, "They fight. That's all they know."

I wanted to keep my dirhams. The coffee which was already brewed and waiting for me at the counter would just have to go to waste. A blond Spanish girl came up to me with her camera. I took a picture of her and her friend, a young Moroccan boy. Lovers. The Moroccan matrons arriving were all decked in expensive d'jellabas of elaborate sequins and embroidery—gold on black or black and white brocade. One had a fur coat, ready for the weather at her destination. These women's high heels jabbed the floor but the good carpet absorbed all dents and sounds. The room was air-conditioned and sound-proofed.

Sprawling white houses and the rectangular minaret on the hill receded in the calm water. The televisions began a new video: rippling sand dunes, kasbah by the sea, mosaic tiles, graceful arches, sloping tagine tops, tribal patterns on ceramics and hennaed hands flashed to the music of western pop. *Come back! Come back to surf, to trek, to wine and dine, to enjoy, to relax, to live your dream vacation like kings and queens in Morocco.*

The ferry docked at Tarifa, a beautiful small Spanish town set against lush green hills and turquoise water. Houses with high arches and columns were painted in soft yellow and salmon colors. Open air restaurants lined the streets. People sat in chairs sipping coffee. All peaceful. No tumbling hustlers to give you big welcome. No garbage in the ditches. No donkey dung. The flies couldn't make it across the water. The sun was warm and the jasmine trees luxuriated. Cows, big fat ones, grazed the hillside. There was not a trace of its neighbor thirty-five minutes across the strait. Here people would not stretch their lips and show their stained or missing teeth uninhibited. No child would tug at your sleeve and ask you to buy tissue papers. Privacy came back like a long lost friend. I slipped into solemn contemplation and stopped smiling.

POEMS

Portals
inspired by Lhasa de Sela

In the beginning
I was a tiny cell
frolicking, tumbling
in a warm, dark sea.

In time I grew hands and feet.
The sea was becoming small.
And soon I felt a supple wall
enfolding, restricting my turns.

One day the wall crumbled
crushed me from all sides.
My painful body was squeezed
down toward a pin of light.

I felt I was dying.
I gasped and grabbed in vain.
And with one final terrifying jolt
I burst into a room of light.

People's laughter, warm blanket
and the comfort of nipple and milk.
I realized instead of dying
I had come to be born.

The world was once again immense
as I stretched my arms and legs.
I climbed the highest mountains
I rode the wildest waves.

But my body began to wither
as the winter sun ashened into night.
My world was gradually reduced
from house, to chair, to bed.

How I struggled to stay alive
with doctor visits and a regimen of drugs,
rare herbs, diets, physical therapy
to slow the inevitable end.

But my heart stopped beating one day,
the bag of skin collapsed.
I could not move my hands or feet
though my mind was raving scared,

until I caught the pin of light
shimmering steadily toward me.
I realized instead of dying
I was about to be born.

Life has no destination,
death has no grip.
The soul journeys through portals
to become a stone, a flower, a bird,

to become the sea, a cloud, the sky,
like nova of a star
to become again
and again.

Suspension

This is the incessant spell of August.

Gaunt faces surface each dreary day
between white bed sheets,
pale, expressionless,
lifting sometimes an elbow,
bending a knee.

At the suggestion of a speech therapist
one drawls childhood's favorite crayons—
how they broke, trampled by feet,
and smeared streaks of colored tracks
down the sidewalk.

The man is somewhat shaved.
Pieces of isolated hair peep
from underneath the chin,
a couple of long ones dangle near the jaw.
His growl annoys the nurse, and in this
incessant spell of August,
his thirst is quenched by an eternal needle.

The spinster picks up
a bowl of grapes and urges
her aunt to taste.
"You have little appetite," she says.
The woman wiggles and squirms
and finally throws up thin green watery paste.

The one in a wheel chair
leans sideways to prevent
himself from sliding down.
In this confining heat
there's no one around
except his wife, who lies still in bed.

Silenced by a stroke,
she can only blink at him.
Neither of them expected August
to drag on this long.

They all look forward to rain.

One of them dreams of an orange moon,
tucked in the lapel of a black tuxedo sky.

A Room In Diyarbakır
November 2011

Turkey—an autumn leaf.

This is the last day of Kurban Bayramı
a religious holiday
commemorating Abraham
sacrificing his only son to God.
Men in suits fill the courtyard.
Women in finery usher in
two young boys
in princely costumes (golden embroidery
on white suits, crowns, capes and scepters).
The sounds of drumming, singing
women ululating—
Between
two fingers
a glow worm
    curls
            "How old are the boys?"
Ma
    smokes
Pa
    smokes
            "Eight and twelve."
High-heeled, manicured sister
with very fine hair
        "She's a jolly chimney."
    smokes.
        "What is the celebration?"
The Imam
    smokes
One for the cut. Two for the screams.
        "Oh, you know, down there."
The drummer
    smokes

The singer
   smokes
The procession is slow coming out.
The guests
   smoke
The waiters
   smoke
      long semi-translucent tunics over the boys' sparkling
white jackets,
but their pants are gone.
     A loud boom in the air.
       A
          shower
   of
         colored
    paper
            petals.
Kurban Bayramı
share what is necessary.
Two-thirds for the poor
one-third to keep.
Cutting of cows and sheep.

Inside a Camii
Kurban Bayramı
the young imam chants.
Men in melodious response
praise Allah, reaffirm faith.

Holiday shopping
a light show in Taksim.
Kurban Bayramı
Plenty of raki
sweet baklavas and honey.

Inside a hotel
five beers two friends and a night mistress
blond hair, red streaks, sturdy as an ox.

Kurban Bayramı
celebrates the flesh.
        I sip
blood-red pomegranate juice
toast to half-bent sister, the crescent moon.

She laughs, her silver teeth tingle my spine
and drench me senseless with the ocean tide.

I lie unclothed on a warm stone,
taste of ambrosia on my tongue.

Her areolas are fruit to my eyes
as she runs her hands over my body and thighs—

*

The Tigris runs shallow,
        A castle ruin atop the hill.
winding idyllically down the canyon.
        At the summit,
Two gigantic stumps, remnants
        weathered tombstones
of an ancient bridge
        dried winter grass.
at a distance upstream.
        A mosque stands at a distance

mosque and tombstones would witness the disappearance of a
village, hundreds of cave dwellings, and the construction of the
dam. "Bon bon, bon bon," local urchins run towards the travel-
ers. Their teeth black like old men's.

I taste sheep in my saliva,
coming into the cold
plains of Mesopotamia.
        Thick,
            thick yogurt in a tub.

Into the bazaar on a donkey's back.
Vegetables and the morning hubbub
Thick, thick yogurt in a tub.
A child sells soap
blackened, dirty soap he salvaged
from the ditches.
At a window
two liras for a cheese pide.
Flats of eggs and a wailing cub.
A busy housewife fills her sack.
Thick, thick yogurt in a tub.
Into the bazaar on a donkey's back.

The café overlooks
a bejeweled minaret
young men sing around a table
laughter takes over
the guitar strums on.
Girl runs down the street
big-eyed girl
no more than five
Allah, Allah
singing her mother's song.
Mother watches in the shadow
her black-haired girl in pink
running down the street
Allah is charitable.
Girl of rosebud face
silver bell voice
girl holding a little plastic tray
no more than five
singing the song Mother taught her
tiny feet pitter-patter
pink tunic flapping
running running Allah Allah
is charitable.
One lira. Mother watches.
One lira. In the shadow.

Mother watches girl running
no more than five.
Plastic slippers, plastic tray
little rosebud, silver bell
Have pity, people, have pity.
The November sun is charitable.
It won't last forever
this, the child, the men, you and me.
The steps of Mardin will survive us all.
Into the lightless alleys, cut-stone walls,
at every bend, the moon.
Your reflection in a night pond
strangely cast,
holding my hand.   ninjas.
                                        flying
                        like
                    walls
                the
Cats scale

morning call to prayer
bleating sheep and donkey hooves
outside the window
Evening
deserted

except for a dreary grocery shop
with miserable looking vegetables.
At a street corner
a lone kebab stand has two customers.
The man rolls up bits of grilled meat
in a piece of bread.
The boy takes off down an alley
into a smoke-filled internet café.
Men and boys sitting in small cubicles bark at each other,
drink tea, play video games. A large sign on the wall

red letters and a big X over a cigarette.

No smoking...something something
1000 lira fine,
something something...
5000 lira fine.

Daylight is quickly fading at 3:30 in the afternoon. I hurry, trying to catch up with Musefa, a Kurd I met at the courtyard of the Olu Camii.

"We have to be quick," Musefa keeps looking at his watch, "The Dengbejs have been singing since morning. They may not stay at the house for very long."

We tread down one alley after another, cobble-stoned streets and high walls on both sides. Soon I lose sight of his back. A young woman appears beside me.

"Dengbej?" She smiles, walks with me to the next corner and points to her left.

A few old men are leaving as we enter the Dengbej house, but return to a room lined with chairs. One begins to sing. His high tenor voice dwells on a pulsated note, each verse ending with an abrupt sigh. He is Pavarotti in a command performance. In his hand is a string of prayer beads he fingers as he sings. When he is finished he shakes our hands and leaves.

Another man begins. His voice low and husky, his pulsating notes more tremulous. As he sings his eyes gleam and his facial expressions are that of ironic resignation—a story of unrequited love...

A few of the Dengbejs are still in the courtyard when the singing is done. One of them comes up to me.

"Chine?"

"Evet."

He speaks, gesticulating, "...helicopter...".

When he finishes he wants Musefa to translate.

"He said the English word "helicopter" came from the Kurdish language. 'Heli' is bird..."

Their oral tradition has few to pass it on. The Dengbejs will carry their music to their graves, then ride in a helicopter to heaven, where all the angels may gather for a feast of song-story.

Night

Musefa's uncle,
     "This is a respectable hotel. No slut."

I close the door.
Residual tremors echo through the building.

Four walls
worn beds
smell of bodies.
The mirror is pride
in the heart of poverty
a cockroach crawls out.
Where am I
is
where I am
there's no toilet paper.
Song-story of love and loss
the old Dengbej sings:
The ocean, the sky, a sheep
I have become
but she doesn't love me.
Pink paint smearing
onto the blue-tiled floor.
The light bulb
naked and bold.
Martyr's images on a TV screen.
Is it such a shock?
The taste of spiced lamb on crisp-baked bread.
The sound of leaking water.
A rippling of dirty white is the window
the plaster an angry slapdash.
The rumbling heater brings some warmth
but comfort is only when I'm fast asleep
dreaming of my father, drowning
(and rescued by my own hands)
instead of imagining the secret police searching

from room to room for PKK sympathizers.
Electricity in mosques and culture centers cut
after sundown.
No call to prayer.
I wait for my escape signal.
It never comes.

*

Murat, god of raki,
you lost my book!
Lord of Sogukçesme,
the glint in your eyes brings me to you.
With dazzling wit
you poke fun at absurdities.
While mortals ponder,
you're gone fishing.

Reappearing at the rooftop kitchen,
chop, dice, grind, shred, stir,
bring down a scrumptious meal to feed a crowd.

Always a crowd.

On a night out you squeeze
seven people into a sedan
and roar into Taksim,
drag a gypsy clarinetist out of his bed.
Then with extended arms
snap fingers,
roll shoulders,
squeal into midnight.

Later, puff smoke like a dragon,
patiently wait for the leaf to return,
to pat you lightly as your mother would
before the first dew
when dreams converse with reality,

the way a tendril
tenderly stretches across the land.

Desolation landscape
dissolves
into glasses of tea.
For every sameness, a sugar cube.
The wind of Marmara flings specks of rain.
Love is a dew drop on the lip.
Night, cold, sits on the bridge.
At the end of the fishing line, a pulse.
"Desire goes out"
despite sleepiness,
"to things as they are in themselves."
A fish, hooked on the roof of its mouth,
writhes.
"Come home," you said.

Note: "Desire goes out to things as they are in themselves."
—St. Thomas Aquinas.

Discovering Clara Hsu:
Babouche Impromptu Plus...
by Jack Foley

"N'importe où hors du monde."
        Charles Baudelaire ("Anywhere out of this world":
Baudelaire is translating the English poet, Thomas Hood)

There are many ways to discover Clara Hsu. She has a book of poems, *Mystique* (2006) and a book of prose sketches, a travel account with the extravagant title, *Babouche Impromptu and Other Moroccan Sketches* (2008). She co-hosts a local poetry television show, *San Francisco Open Mic Poetry Podcast TV Show* (formerly *Mystic Babylon Poetry Podcast*), with her friend, poet/videographer John Rhodes, and you can find a number of her performances on YouTube. (She recites in Chinese as well as English.) She has a CD, *The Mystical Path*, which features her performance partner, Bill Mercer, along with herself—as well as shakuhachi flute and drum played by Mercer and Hsu. (On one track she sings, tenderly and beautifully—though she is quick to point out that she is not a "professional" singer.) She has a website, http://www.clarahsu.com. She calls her San Francisco home The Poetry Hotel and hosts a monthly salon there. Poetry for her is intensely communal.

Her personal history is interesting. Born in Hong Kong—her father manufactured pianos—she began as a musician. (She still teaches piano.) In 1982 she founded with her father the world music shop, Clarion Music Center in San Francisco's Chinatown. The store, whose name puns on "Clara," has been described as "not your ordinary music store," "full of instruments, especially Chinese ones & music of many cultures." The store continues to thrive, though she and her father are no longer the owners. She is restless, intelligent, imaginative, sometimes surprisingly and fearlessly assertive, capable of extravagant, life-changing gestures that annihilate what most likely struck her as boring stability: In "February 2007," she writes, "I sold

my business, ended a long marriage [which had produced two
children] and became a poet. I studied Arabic for a year and re-
turned to Morocco, this time alone." She practices, she says, "the
art of multidimensional being." *Mystique* concludes with "Away":

> *As soon as you walk in the door*
> *you will find I've already gone*
>
> *to a mountain sits amid*
> *a void and aimless drifting clouds*
>
> *drunk with elixir*
> *the tarnished silver sphere reminisces*
>
> *I leave you a roomful of memories*
> *do what you want with them.*

*

Babouche Impromptu is a book of memories. The sketches
are not unlike those Christopher Isherwood produced in Berlin
Stories. Like Isherwood's, Hsu's speaker might say, "I am a camera."
She is there more as a presence—a point of view—than as a
"person":

> *Hassan the receptionist woke up when he heard me drag-*
> *ging my luggage down the stairs. His eyes were puffy with sleep.*
> *"When you come back, remember this is your home."*
>
> *I thanked him and walked to the square. D'jamaa Elfna*
> *stood empty of activities. The grounds had been cleaned. Puddles*
> *of water reflected the early morning light. A couple of snakes and*
> *men idled at their usual spot. They were the only remnant from*
> *yester-night.*
>
> *A taxi was waiting. The driver approached. I asked him*
> *how much it would cost to go to the bus station.*
> *"Twenty dirhams," he said.*
> *I shook my head and kept walking.*

"Fifteen dirhams," he yelled.
Another taxi pulled up. This time I told the driver through
the open window how much I would pay. He nodded and I got in.

The prose is simple, direct. It never insists on what
"Clara" feels—though we realize that, despite the fact that her
luggage is heavy ("dragging my luggage down the stairs"), she is
not going to pay an extravagant price for that taxi ride. Finally,
her will prevails: "This time I told the driver through the open
window how much I would pay."

The sketches are always charming, easy to read, filled
with interesting details. There is even a sprinkling of Arabic
throughout the book. (We learn, among other things, how to say
"thank you": *shukran*.) *Babouche Impromptu* concentrates on *the*
other, and if, at least in part, the initial appeal of the other is its
exoticism, Hsu works hard to diminish that exoticism, to bring
the other into the realm of deliberate human interaction. Asked
if he will pose for a photograph, one of the people she encounters
answers, "I'm not...strange thing you bring back America...No,
no, we're not, er...exotique!" Of course he is exotique, but Hsu's
sincere interest and compassionate curiosity allow us to experi-
ence such characters as vivid and understandable: each, we know,
has his or her "reasons"—and of course an historical/national
context in which he or she exists. In this sense Hsu's book might
be described as a *reclamation* of the exotic other.

Yet there is another, more lyrical strain to *Babouche Im-*
promptu. It surfaces in deliberately "purple" passages like this—
though even here "objective" description is a strong factor:

D'jamaa Elfna—the pulse of my heart. Your air is per-
fumed with incense mixed with the smell of grilled meat. Motor-
bikes criss-crossing, among pedestrians, blind beggars' sing-song
in the midst of flowing robes, and snake charmers' circular arm
motions bring me to you.

The strain also surfaces in the subdued theme of eroticism

which echoes throughout the book. Here is one instance:

> *The storyteller's voice spiraled and pounded in my direc-*
> *tion as though he was questioning me. His husky and seductive*
> *litany touched a darkness that was lurking as I saw myself coming*
> *upon a solitary adobe hut, small, round, ashen against the night.*
> *As I walked toward it, the storyteller's voice turned strident.*
> *..I can't go in...there's no door, no window...it's a funeral*
> *mound...*
> *He was now whispering, urging.*
>
> *Our eyes met.*
>
> *I stepped back.*

In another, a man "pulls me forward and presses his
lips on my cheeks." The—climax—of this theme is "Threesome
with Jack Kerouac," a delightful and utterly fanciful chapter in
which Hsu finds herself in bed with the long-dead author of *On
the Road*. Nothing explicit is offered, but the reader's imagina-
tion is allowed to toy with various possibilities, especially since
Hsu does kiss the famous author's cheek as she snuggles next
to him. There is of course always an erotic element to travel, to
encountering the other—so, while surprising, the chapter does
connect with the general theme of the book. Yet it also suggests
that eroticism is one of the deep sources of Clara Hsu's restless,
off-flying imagination—the power that allowed her to sell her
business, end a long marriage, become a poet, and journey alone
to Morocco. A recent poem describing a Turkish *religious* festival
concludes,

> *Inside a hotel*
> *five beers two friends and a night mistress*
> *blond hair, red streaks, sturdy as an ox.*
> *Kurban Bayramı*
> *celebrate the flesh.*

N'importe où hors du monde. The kind of eroticism embodied in *Babouche Impromptu* can easily rise to the realm of mysticism ("*mystique*").

*

The encounter with the other postulates a self to which the other has reference. The natural mode of this encounter is necessarily descriptive—we need to know that the other is other—and the entire enterprise remains in the realm of subject/object (I/*Thou*).

In her most recent work, Clara Hsu seems to have moved away from that mode—though she has certainly not abandoned it. The most spectacular example of a stylistic change in her work is "From Dallas to Istanbul." In this tour de force, description remains but it is only one element in a structure which is essentially an interplay of voices—the self not as a sounding board for a perceived other but as a potpourri, a multiplicity, the center of an ongoing chaos of yackety-yak that arises from *both* "inside" and "outside." Travel remains—we are in an airport—but who exactly is the "me" at the end of the poem?

"Boarding First Class Passengers."
  Will the elite please be seated.
    "Don't you know me by now? I really don't care."

Boy bouncing up and down on the automatic walkway.
  Starbucks' Earl Gray. Gulp it down. Tall, Grande, Venti, whatever—lifestyle, sophistication—they mean.
    "Turkish tea, apple tea, Nescafe?"

Line forming. Into the tunnel of no return.
  All we like sheep, have (not) gone astray...husbands, wives, friends, lovers, businessmen, doctors, lawyers, architects, contractors, teachers, musicians, artists, babies. Poet.
    "People!"

129

Old man with breasts. Backpack, shorts, tennis shoes.
   My father's breasts are naturally aged.
      "My hands on yours..."

Beep. You passed. Beep. Beep.
   How many affairs do you need? Who's keeping score? Have I
passed? Am I a poet now?
      "Get a life, you say?"

The corridor is strangely quiet.
   Like the heart. It knows.
      "I knew from the moment I set eyes on you."

Caution. Slippery when wet.
   Words.
      "Voices!"

Oneworld.
   One. The body is an extension of the mind and it is beautiful.
      "I love you I love you I..."

The stewardess cannot (will not) help you with your luggage.
   Suddenly there are two worlds. Us vs. them.
      "We cannot get rid of the people around us, those boring, dull
people who rob us the pleasures of life."

"Did you order a special meal?" she asked, coldly.
   What about drugs? Never tried though got high on second
hand pot smoke once. My daughter's boyfriend told me to eat some
psychedelic mushrooms. A few bites would take me into the altered
state.
      "mmm...more...you."

"Fasten your seatbelt." The machine said. It's all machine from
Dallas to Istanbul.
   Peter, we must meet up after your session with Hilary Clinton. I
understand. Work first. But S.F—D.C.—IST! What synchronistic
serendipity!

"*And we must get used to not being together.*"

signed, me.

Hsu is a musician: if the work we see in *Babouche Impromptu* tends to be duets—two people talking—this work is *fugal*. It opens us to the polyvocal nature of the world. (Each of the lines is itself a mélange of voices.)

Another recent poem that moves in a similar direction—though it is stylistically less adventuresome than "From Dallas to Istanbul"—is "Things That Are and Things That Dream." The poem has an oneiric quality that puts a definite haint on the various "things" which would have been so carefully (and objectively) presented in *Babouche Impromptu*:

Cool air rushes in from an open window.
The curtain fringes waver: yes/no.
Gulls cry
like babies in distress. Such sorrow as they
circle a slow dance above the minarets.

Inside Sinan's courtyard
his handprints heavy under each ancient brick.

Shape of a tulip
a young girl with headscarf, her long waist leaning
for a butterfly kiss.

The half moon
separates things that are and things that dream
holds them upon her face.

The cobblestone street
whoever walked here today has appeared and disappeared.

Earlier on, an orange cat put his paws on my knees.

You said it is in search of love.
I said it is lonely.

Things that are
have no need for us.

Things that dream
are what we're made of.

Babouche Impromptu deals with "things that are." Here, everything exists in a world larger than any individual thing's particularities. The poem suggests that there is a deep sorrow at the heart of the world—and that nothing is solid: "whoever walked here today has appeared and disappeared." Though the poem abounds with description, "we" are at distance from everything it names. Loneliness colors everything, turns everything into a metaphor for sorrow. Here, the world is a dream, and we are only dreamers:

Things that are
have no need for us.

*

As a Chinese-American woman living in San Francisco, Clara Hsu has undoubtedly encountered the "attraction of the exotic": there are surely plenty of Western men who think of Chinese-American women as exotic—something out of the "mysterious East." Yet when Hsu writes about exoticism she does not write about herself as an exotic object of desire—as many Asian feminists might. Rather, *she* is the person experiencing the "exotic." Everything in *Babouche Impromptu* is a testing of her own capacity for understanding and sympathy. How can she present this "exotic" material as something real and even (which it also is) everyday? How can she deal not with the objectification of herself, as a feminist might, but with her own tendencies towards objectification? The vividness of her book is a wonderful indication of her success.

Yet the issues raised by objectification remain in the realm of subject/object, and Hsu is an artist whose deep imagination is in a constant state of movement. "Life," she writes, "has no destination,"

> *death no grip.*
> *The soul journeys through portals*
> *to become a stone, a flower, a bird,*
> *to become the sea, a cloud, the sky,*
> *like nova of a star*
> *to become again*
> *and again.* ("Portals")

Identity is not fixed but constantly changing. It is constantly *away.* Someone remarked to Charles Olson that he "went all around the subject." Olson answered that he didn't know it was a subject. Hsu does not wish to limit herself any more than Olson did, though, as in Baudelaire, boredom—*Ennui, stoppage*—is a continual threat:

> *Gaunt faces surface each dreary day*
> *between white bed sheets,*
> *pale, expressionless,*
> *lifting sometimes an elbow,*
> *bending a knee.* ("Suspension")

How can one assert one's freedom, challenge and repudiate reality if not by acts of audacity and bravery? Clara Hsu's answers to this question constitute her art, her poetry, her mode of "multidimensional being":

Oneworld.

One. The body is an extension of the mind and it is beautiful.

*

Discovering Clara Hsu is an ongoing process—and I do not mean to suggest that the process has come to an end. She has already produced some extraordinary work, and I'm sure that more is on the way. Everything I say here is necessarily tentative, to be continued, even contradicted. (I have not yet shown the piece to the lady herself.) But I want to end this essay with Clara Hsu's gorgeous translation, "Farewell, River Cam," from the Chinese of the early twentieth century master, Xu Zhimo (1897-1931), one of the first poets to bring Western Romantic forms into Chinese. One may celebrate movement, energy, and freedom, one may celebrate the beauty of the other as one encounters it in the here and now, and yet elegy—even nostalgia—may be an aspect of that celebration.

> *I leave softly*
> *as I come,*
> *quietly wave*
> *farewell to the clouds.*
> *By the river, the golden willow*
> *is the bride of sunset.*
> *Her reflection undulates,*
> *sways in my heart.*
> *Moss on soft mud*
> *washes gleaming on the riverbed.*
> *Let me be a weed*
> *in the gentle river Cam.*
> *The pond glistens under the shade*
> *it is not a cascade,*
> *but a rainbow*
> *broken up among the rushes,*
> *immersed in illusory dreams.*
> *Finding dreams? Take a long pole,*
> *steer towards the greenest grass.*
> *Fill the boat with starlight,*
> *give song in the midst of shimmer.*
> *But I have no song.*
> *Silence is the wind of parting.*
> *Crickets are keeping still,*
> *tonight, the river is hushed.*
> *I leave softly*
> *as I come,*

dusting the sleeves,
not taking a piece of cloud.

POSTSCRIPT 2013

The current edition of *Babouche Impromptu* contains writing that was not in the original edition; when I wrote the above remarks, I had read only the original edition. The section dealing with the Sahara and with Youssef has been added for this book.

I suggested above that eroticism was a "subdued theme" that echoed throughout the book. In this new section, eroticism is far from subdued: it is the central issue, and the author's I-am-a-camera persona is dropped in favor of a Clara who becomes an actor in her story. The Sahara material makes it clear that, whether she fully understood it or not, the author was going to Morocco to find love, and that included physical love—though she does not wish to fully confront that aspect of her longing. Youssef—along with the entirety of the desert—is an immense erotic temptation. I think that what Hsu is calling "the Sahara" is in fact an exoticized version of her own Eros, an Eros which brings her into a situation in which physical love—Eros as sexuality—vies with an Eros which is sublimated into "the spirit of Sahara reaching out, embracing its long-lost daughter." Hsu asserts that "the gift of love was bestowed upon me"—but what sort of love is it? The presence of Youssef and his longing is a distinct reminder that Eros cannot be so easily sublimated into

The Moon is your mother.
The sun is your father.
The desert is your home.

Throughout the Youssef episode, we understand the author's ambivalence towards this young Berber. One feels that Hsu desires Youssef—there are sparks—but the only thing Youssef can truly offer this sophisticated, self-realizing woman is the kind of life his mother leads, a life which is far from anything she would wish for herself. Still, desire is desire. As they part, Youssef kisses Clara tenderly:

> *His hand slowly touched my hair, neck, and down toward my chest. I cupped it before it went any further. He lowered his eyes, hiding a mixture of longing and disappointment.*

She then gives him the address of her hotel in Marrakech. She adds, "The thought of Youssef weaved in and out of my mind. Did I reciprocate his affection?" Alone in her room, "during the night when someone knocked loudly on the hotel door, I wondered if it was he, and whether our encounter would have further meaning beyond the Sahara."

One can't know for certain, but the reader feels that had Youssef shown up at the hotel room, Clara would finally have said yes to him—if only for that night. It is possible that a kind of cultural misunderstanding was taking place. Clara was perhaps *testing* Youssef, telling him, *I know you want me, but are you willing to wait, to put off your wanting for a little while?* But Youssef may have been testing Clara, too—or at least asking her a question. Because she prevents him from touching her breast—because she frustrates him—he believes that she would do the same thing at the hotel. He would make the trip and be frustrated once again. So he doesn't show up. But it may be that they were involved in a clash of cultures: she believed she was telling him, *Wait*, but he believed she was telling him, *No*. In any case, "I did not see Youssef again."

But that is not quite the end of the story. Though she did not make love to Youssef, she did accept the turban/scarf he gave her, and she wears it frequently to this day. It is, she says, her "signature attire." The scarf is a love-token of a relationship that might have become physical but didn't. It seems to symbolically represent the author's complex feelings about the Sahara and her adventures there. Because the scarf is long, it sometimes has the appearance of a river that flows around her body. But it is also *gold,* and she wears it nearly every day: it is like a wedding ring.

—Jack Foley

Babouche Impromptu Plus... was first published in *The Alsop Review,* November 18, 2011; and again in *The Tower Journal,* January, 2012.

Jack Foley is an innovative poet and critic who, with his wife, Adelle, performs his work frequently in the San Francisco Bay Area.

About the Author

Clara Hsu practices the art of multi-dimensional being: mother, musician, purveyor of Clarion Music Center (1982-2005), traveler, translator and poet.

A nominee for the Pushcart Prize in poetry (2001), Clara's first book of poems, *Mystique*, received honorable mention at the 2010 San Francisco Book Festival. *Babouche Impromptu and Other Moroccan sketches* was completed in 2008. Her work can be found in *New Millennium Writings* (2012), *Hafenklänge, Havenklanken—Sounds of Harbor* (translations of her work into Dutch and German), *The Haight-Ashbury Literary Journal,* and the internet journals *Cha, The Other Voices International Project, and Tower Journal.* She was the featured poet in the 33rd issue of the British poetry journal, *Erbacce.*

Clara gives featured readings at various Bay Area venues and benefit events, often in collaboration with others such as Bill Mercer and Jack and Adelle Foley. Her activities include her unusual performance ensemble "Lunation," which combines Chinese and original poetry with Asian traditional instruments. For seven years she hosted the Poetry Hotel Salon in San Francisco and with John Rhodes she co-hosts the San Francisco Open Mic Poetry Podcast TV Show.